NEVER ALONE

The Story of Victory During the Cultural Revolution

Authors: Drs. Timothy and Pearl Yeh
Co-Author: Janet Yeh

INTERNATIONAL DISTRIBUTORS

Christ The Way Publications, Inc.
P.O. Box 43120, Eastwood Square
Kitchener, Ont. N5H 6S9, Canada

B. McCall Barbour
28 George IV Bridge
Edinburgh, Scotland/UK EH1 1ES
Tel: 031-225 4816

New Zealand Evangelistic Society
P.O. Box 50096
Porirua, Wellington, New Zealand

Evangelistic Literature Enterprise
P.O. Box 5010
Brendale, Q'ld., Australia 4500
Tel: (07) 3205-7100

Gospel Publishers
P.O. Box 1
Westhoven 2142, South Africa
Tel: (11) 673-3157
Fax: (11) 673-2644

Sword Distributors
P.O. Box 3459
Parklands 2121, South Africa
Tel/Fax: (11) 486-3361

Chick Gospel Literatur
Postfach 1166
D-51387 Burscheid
Germany
Tel. 02174/63815
Fax: 02174/2799

Copyright © 1997
by Drs. Timothy and Pearl Yeh

All rights reserved. No part of this book may be reproduced, stored in a retrieval system or transmitted in any form or by any means (electronic, mechanical, photocopying, recording or otherwise) without permission in writing from the copyright owner.

ISBN: 0-937958-56-5

222/A   *First Revised Edition*

Published by Chick Publications
P.O. Box 662, Chino, CA 91708-0662 USA
Tel: (909) 987-0771 • Fax: (909) 941-8128

http://chick.com
E-Mail: postmaster@chick.com

Printed in the United States of America

Introduction

Ever since we met... the author, his wife, and I... in their homeland, I have had troublesome thoughts that will not go away and disturbing questions that will not be stilled. Such as...

What makes them so different anyway?

Is it that they have reached beyond themselves for those resources it takes to be real Christians anywhere?

Have those same divine resources not only enabled them to survive a literal hell on earth but also made them incredibly strong?

Can you decide to do that without being forced to? ...to actually get into a commitment you can't handle without God's help? ... when something divine simply has to happen?

Is my commitment requiring much divine to happen or can I pretty well handle myself?

Do only those Christians who undergo severe persecution achieve their level of faith... that qualify their depth of commitment... or is it open to anyone else? If so, what are the terms?

Must I be deprived of that privilege simply because I happen to live in a society that has let me be a Christian so far without too much pressure... and with nothing you could call sacrifice?

I sure wish I had been praying more for them. I will from now on. That is a promise.

I just wonder if I would risk my life for my Bible, not to mention my songbook.

I want to learn more about gratitude.

I want to learn more about faith and obedience and courage. But do I really?

And finally, *"Must I be carried to the skies on flowery beds of ease, while others fought to win the prize and sailed through bloody seas?"*

So as you move through these pages you will be confronted with a new and serious spiritual challenge. And you will clearly hear God's promise again:

> *Strength for the day,*
> *Rest for the labor,*
> *Light for the way,*
> *Grace for the trials,*
> *Help from above,*
> *Unfailing sympathy,*
> *Undying love.*

Dr. Paul Skiles
Executive Director of Communications
for the Church of the Nazarene

Contents

Introduction

Chapter 1 - Background 7

Chapter 2 - The Cultural Revolution Hits Home 13

Chapter 3 - What Happened in My Family 31

Chapter 4 - Life in Prison 47

Chapter 5 - Deepening Persecution 65

Chapter 6 - Ignored and Attacked Again 83

Chapter 7 - Life in a Prison Hospital 101

Chapter 8 - Under House Arrest 111

Chapter 9 - Pearl – My Wife's Story 125

Chapter 10 - Eight Years of Political Discrimination . .151

Chapter 11 - Led by God 167

Chapter 12 - America 181

Chapter 13 - Growing Through Suffering 195

Chapter 14 - The Battle With the Devil in America. . .209

Chapter 15 - Faith and Final Words 215

Drs. Pearl and Timothy Yeh

1

Background

This is a book about survival during the Cultural Revolution, which hit China from 1967 to 1977. There was no law at all in China. The attack was led by communist Chairman Mao Tse-Tung and the Gang of Four political party. Mao Tse-Tung's wife (Jiang Qin) and three political high officers made up the Gang of Four. Chairman Mao was the head of law. He wiped out all the laws in the Chinese constitution that he could not profit from.

They believed in complete dictatorship and total control of the minds and actions of the Chinese people. They believed in no freedom of religion, no Western contact, no individualism, no capitalism, and no intellectual thinking. Most importantly, they tolerated no one who was against Mao's laws, his thinking, and his acts. Anyone who engaged in the activities the government did not approve, was considered a criminal to be imprisoned, tortured, or even shot. Thus, criminals fell into one of two categories. The first group were the criminals who murdered, raped, and robbed. The government didn't consider them to be real criminals, but rather light cases. The second category consisted of political prisoners, who were considered severe criminals by the government. These people were scientists, scholars, artists, writers, Christians, Catholics, landlords, and capitalists. Some of them possessed wealth, had relatives and friends from abroad, were involved with or worked for another political party before 1949, belonged to the bourgeois class or had different political beliefs.

During the Cultural Revolution, there were mainly two classes of people in the Chinese society. Led by Chairman Mao, the Gang of Four took advantage of the proletarian (working) class and the peasants. Those belonging to the proletarian class did not own any land or property, nor were they educated. The Gang of Four upheld this class, because they were the majority and this allowed the government to exercise complete control. With no wealth, no education, no status, the proletarian was easily called and used by the government. Therefore, as long as a citizen was proletarian, he/she was considered a good person.

Since Maosim did not desire that the masses be educated, it spread rampantly and quickly particularly among the young. Students in elementary, middle, high school, and college were stirred up to go out to public parks and meeting places, and discouraged from attending school. They were filled with excitement and happiness in not having to study.

However, if a citizen was from the bourgeois class, they were considered to be a dangerous element against the government. The Gang of Four tortured this class, which included Christians, Catholics, college graduates, thinkers, doctors, teachers, scholars, politicians, professional people, and those with wealth. Because much of the science and advanced research was coming from Western cultures, the bourgeois class often came into contact with Western customs and religion, such as Christianity, different clothing, Western books and publications. They also had friends from America, Europe, and Hong Kong.

Our families were caught in the midst of this chaos, and our lives turned upside down. We were from the bourgeois class.

My father was a chemist who graduated from Shanghai University in China, and along with his two brothers, were the founders of the perfume industry in all of China. They owned much land, had resorts, factories, and hotels in various cities. My mother was an education major and was a classmate of my father at the same university. After she married my father, she didn't need to work, but rather managed the house and her family and saw to the education of her children. I am the youngest of three children and have two older brothers.

I was raised in a Christian home, so I knew Jesus when I was little. In 1952, when I was fifteen, an evangelist came from the north to our city, Shanghai.

He preached about repentance and receiving the Holy Spirit, so my brothers and I repented and were born again. I dedicated myself before the Lord in order that I would serve Him all my life. If God would call me for His work, I promised Him that my answer would be "Yes!" and that living for Him would be the goal of my life. But unfortunately, the door of the gospel of Christianity grew narrower and narrower. And there was no possibility for me to do as I desired.

When I was growing up, I loved languages, such as English, German, Japanese, and Chinese, so I studied diligently four languages and the sciences. When I was around seventeen and in high school, my parents asked me to learn natural medicine before attending medical school. The reason they suggested that I do so was because my mother was stricken with severe illnesses twice in her life that almost caused her death. At the hospital, top level doctors that graduated from Japan, Germany, America, France, and England couldn't save her life. They asked my father and grandfather to take her back home and prepare for the funeral. But during her life's two critical moments, she was saved by natural medicine.

At nineteen years of age, I entered medical university to study modern medicine, where I translated many articles from Japanese into Chinese for medical journals in China. I became proud of my little successes in medicine. After years of study in two fields of medicine, I passed the board test to practice natural medicine and modern medicine. At the Children's Hospital in 1963, I got an invitation from the Japanese Acupuncture Association to attend an international conference as a speaker. I was excited and reported to our medical chief in order to get government approval to speak at the conference. I didn't know it at the time, but this later became one of the incriminations the government laid on me during the Cultural Revolution. They accused me of being a traitor and a Japanese spy.

There was another incrimination by the government during this time. I had an aunt and uncle in America. My uncle had a chemical factory in Hong Kong manufacturing wig fibers for America and he knew that I majored in chemistry after medical school. My aunt offered me a position as an engineer in their factory and asked me to apply to leave China, and I did so. However, my application was denied two times before 1965. So the government accused me of being a traitor and a Western spy. To tell the truth, if my application had been approved, I would have left my homeland because we all had the terrible feeling that Maoism would destroy my whole family and collapse all of China.

My wife was a concert pianist, and a graduate of the Peking Conservatory. She performed for prominent government officials. She studied English and Russian, as well as Chinese. She often traveled and performed on the piano and accordion. Her father was a businessman, who had travelled to Japan. On his return, he would bring home Western arts, sculptures, fabrics, and publications. He also had contact with officials in the nationalist government. He was arrested three years after the communists took over China and died in prison. My wife's mother became a teacher and raised five children on her single income after her husband's death.

In just a few days, the Gang of Four took away everything that we had labored for our entire lives. Even though we had committed no wrongs, our possessions were burned, our properties were confiscated, family members were beaten, and my wife and I were both thrown into the prison. The reasons for their actions were that, we were a Christian family, we were intellectuals, we had friends and relatives in America and Hong Kong, and we were from the bourgeois class.

During our weakest moments, God was with us and beside us. We could only turn to Him for direction and help. We learned important lessons and experienced the meaning of being a true Christian, even unto death.

2

The Cultural Revolution Hits Home

The Cultural Revolution actually began in 1955 when the political air spread quickly into bigger cities all over China. Fear was in the air. People were frightened at being criticized, tortured, arrested, and even killed. Suicide was common.

Bang! Bang! Bang! "Open the door. Open the door." It was nine o'clock in the evening of August 24, 1966. The pounding was loud and rough. Stones, bricks, sticks, and mud were thrown against our house. The windows of my house were broken one by one. We had never experienced anything like this. It was one of the sudden attacks organized by the "Red Guards." They numbered about 15 million throughout China, mainly high school and college students but supported and backed up by the Central Committee. They attacked the bourgeois class, the class of scholars and professionals, and uplifted the proletarian class. It was the beginning to what the world came to know as the "Cultural Revolution."

We leaped out of bed quaking with fear, wondering what was happening. We could see the street below was filled with angry high school students wearing red arm bands printed with yellow Chinese characters, RED GUARDS.

"Open the door," they shouted. "Quick, you rotten troublemakers."

The door was smashed even while we were hurrying to open it. They rushed into our house like the flood of lava from a volcano, screaming, "Down with the bourgeois class. Down with all exploiter elements. You slaves of Western culture and science, get out of this house. It is time to put an end to all of you. Hands up! Surrender!"

We asked, "What is going on? What law have we broken? Why are you doing this?"

"Shut up," they answered. "You have no right to speak. You have no right to ask questions. Take out all of your treasures and keys. Surrender all your official papers and letters. Do you know who we are? We are Red Guards guided directly by our great leader. We are here to search your house."

We quickly picked up a copy of the *Constitution of the People's Republic of China* to argue with them. We said, "We are a law abiding family living here together with our parents. We work as doctors and college professors. Since we have broken no law, you cannot search our house. This is the law."

One of the guards grabbed the copy of the

constitution and threw it back into our faces, saying, "How stupid can you be? If you dare resist us, you are breaking the law. We have authority to put you into prison. Will you challenge us? Mao's word is the law now. Do you dare to challenge it? You must obey!"

Then about fifty guards scattered into all the rooms of the house. They forced our family into one room, with four officers sitting at the door to guard us. We were forbidden to talk. We were allowed no food, no water, no bathroom visits, and no fans. All we could do was to ask God to save us from injury and to close their eyes to what they should not discover while searching the house that could be used to prosecute us.

We could plainly hear the sounds of the search. Doors opened... trunks and cases overturned and smashed... drawers pulled out and emptied. They were digging into the floors, hammering on walls, and drilling into them. The intruders even climbed to the roof to turn up the tiles. The Guards shouted with glee when they discovered money or something of value. They scolded loudly if a drawer yielded nothing that they wanted.

Their ransacking included not only the inside of the house, but also outside in the yard. They destroyed flowers and plants, digging one hole after another thinking we might have buried treasures to conceal them. They wrote graffiti on the walls of our three story house, with slogans such as "Down with the Western slaves and the bourgeois class." and "Long live the Cultural Revolution." Our house and yard looked like a battlefield.

The surprise search included all our treasures – jewels, gold, silver, and money. Our greatest concern was that the Guards were looking for documents, letters, certificates, samples of handwriting, and even small handwritten notes – hoping to find proofs to support their false charges against us. They hoped to take away our belongings on the pretense that we were guilty of a crime against Chairman Mao or the government. If they could find and destroy titles to the property and certificates of ownership, we would be without legal defense when they confiscated our property and took us to trial.

My father had brought great profits to the government through his scientific endeavors in the natural perfume industry. All of his children had worked hard. We had been especially careful to obey the regulations of the government, knowing we were suspect because we were not born into a proletarian family. Suddenly we were treated as political criminals. We had committed no crimes and had broken no law. Unfortunately, the law had been canceled in one night. Huddled together in that room, we worried deeply about what they might find and what they would do to us. That night we thought we knew how Jesus' disciples must have felt when *"there arose a great storm of wind, and the waves beat into the ship, so that it was now full."* (Mark 4:37)

The Cultural Revolution Hits Home

At that mad time almost anything that reflected prosperity or Western culture made one suspect: leather shoes of good quality or modern style, ladies' skirts, dresses, and stockings, men's suits and neckties, any pictures or photos found in nonproletarian families, classic Eastern or Western literature, novels, records, tapes, radios, T.V. sets, refrigerators, furniture, fountain pens, watches, all Western magazines and newspapers, even Western scientific books – all made one an enemy of the Cultural Revolution.

Our home was searched and ransacked by the Red Guards every day for two weeks. Nothing remained concealed and nothing of value was left. The Guards burned all of our books, diplomas, certificates, documents, drawings, curios, photos, Bibles, and hymn books. Even though they could not be used to incriminate us, they also destroyed ancient Chinese relics and Western mementos.

These Red Guards in their teens destroyed everything that they thought to be useless. But they were too young to know much about what was valuable. They were badly taught and rushed rampant into homes of suspected enemies of the Cultural Revolution. This searching and destroying was called, "Totally Destructive Home Searching."

The Red Guards sat in the windows or on balconies singing and laughing while they threw our shoes, clothing, furniture, books, and albums into the fire. They shouted loudly, "Long live our leader Mao and our vice leader Lin. Long live the Cultural Revolution. Long live the Red Guards."

At the end of these two weeks, our material possessions of a lifetime were gone. My retired parents were each given only 12 yuan (about $10.00) per month to live on. It was a rude shock after being accustomed to the comforts of a professional life and a middle-class income. There was physical stress and mental tension, with no hope for improvement in the future. Life was difficult but we felt fortunate at the close of each day that we were all together; none of us were in prison. However, we always felt that our lives were in danger.

Our parents worried about their children, and the children worried about their parents' safety. We knew many people who were put into prison immediately simply because the Guards found one sentence in an old letter from a friend that they considered against the present government. Others suffered the same fate when a legal title to property owned under the former government was discovered in their files. This supposedly proved that they wished the return of the former government. Some small excuse could always be found to justify their sudden attack and to prove their charges.

For example, my oldest brother loved to collect stamps and coins ever since he was very young. These stamps, coins, and cash pieces were often from Western countries or they had the head of a former president or official from a nationalist government. That was the basis of the Red Guards' persecution. They incriminated my brother with phrases such as, "Hating communist government in your mind." or "Expecting Western capitalist and nationalist governments' return." My brother and the entire family was tortured a great deal because of this.

It seemed that everything was gone, but we had Jesus living inside us. Every night we knelt together in the presence of God asking for His protection. Wonderfully He delivered us from dangers one by one. Through our earnest prayers, God shut our persecutors' eyes to some personal papers that were entirely legal but which would have been used against us. At the same time, God comforted our hearts even while we were in great sorrow. The more we tasted bitter persecution, the more we felt sweetness from above.

What God Taught Me

Out of these experiences God opened my eyes and my heart to understand what He was doing for His own. He made us see clearly that all the worldly treasures and successes for which men had labored many generations could be taken away within hours. Many upper class Chinese people who did not believe in Jesus could not take these heavy losses. They fell ill after their possessions were taken away and many committed suicide. They would tell their family members, "There is no reason to live anymore."

Our losses taught me the truths that James knew: *"Go to now, ye rich men, weep and howl for your miseries that shall come upon you. Your riches are corrupted, and your garments are motheaten. Your gold and silver is cankered; and the rust of them shall be a witness against you, and shall eat your flesh as it were fire. Ye have heaped treasure together for the last days."* (James 5:1-3) I began to understand how wise our parents had been when they stored most of their properties in heaven. They had taken care of God's children in troubles and had given happily for the support of the church.

My mother proudly pointed out to us, "Sons, God has revealed to me long ago that things in this world could not stay forever with me. We shouldn't deposit in a bank in the world. We should deposit what we have in heaven. I have followed this and this is why the Red Guards could not find what they had hoped for. My possessions are in heaven, where they cannot search, rob and take away. I am happy no one can take away from my heavenly bank the things I have given to God. God's Word is the truth. We live for Him. Don't be scared. God will help us."

I realized that if we Christians worked only for our own living, it was unworthy and meaningless. I came to understand that being a good Christian did not mean wealth, material goods, education, and status, but rather faith and obedience to God. I perceived that God's Word will not be changed – not even one dash or one dot. I admonished myself that I should esteem my spiritual life more than my medical career – though medicine seemed to me a very valuable work.

I began to repent of my sins of worldly pursuits and of neglecting God's will in my life. I examined myself to recollect all the wrongs that I had committed, and asked for God's forgiveness. The more I repented, the more light I saw. I praised God and thanked Him for His goodness and His justice. He taught me the truths of the Bible: *"And when he is come, he will reprove the world of sin, and of righteousness, and of judgment."* (John 16:8) Also, *"For the time is come that judgment must begin at the house of God."* (I Peter 4:17) My spirit said, Amen. We were His. We belonged to His household. God used all of this to help us know His love and His justice, for *"we know that all things work together for good to them that love God, to them who are the called according to his purpose."* (Romans 8:28) This was the understanding that came from above. The truth made us happy even in sorrow. We trusted Him and we obeyed Him.

One of Satan's master strokes is to keep Christian people silent. He thus robs the world of the Good News and hinders people from finding Christ. The "Gang of Four" knew this and they tried to shut off all Christian influences. During the 1960's, the churches in China were closed. Bibles and hymn books were burned everywhere they were found. Preachers, staff members, and responsible lay brothers and sisters were arrested or forced to do heavy labor. There could be no public worship, no preaching or praying, no reading of Scripture or Christian teaching, no singing or winning new believers. Nevertheless, silent and private prayers were offered to God by His true children everywhere. I have seen now that God was cleansing the Christians' minds and opening the believers' spirits to sanctification.

I knew how the Psalmist felt, and I always sighed deeply when I remembered Psalms 137:1-2, 5-6: *"By the rivers of Babylon, there we sat down, yea we wept, when we remembered Zion. We hanged our harps upon the willows in the midst thereof. If I forget you, O Jerusalem, let my right hand forget her cunning. If I do not remember thee, let my tongue cleave to the roof of my mouth; if I prefer not Jerusalem above my chief joy."*

In these days we needed the strength that comes from God's Word, but the only access we had was what we could recall. I regretted greatly that I had not memorized more precious verses when I had a Bible to read. I am afraid when we have God's blessings we do not esteem them as highly as we should. After we came to the United States, an American pastor told me, "You never know how forgetful our church members are. They remember today what I preached about, but they forget about it in the following weeks." During the Cultural Revolution, I learned to never take God for granted, to never take prayer for granted, and never to take His Word, the Bible, for granted.

The Red Guards always ridiculed us boldly, "Where is your God now? If God knows you, why does He not come to save you? If you still believe, you had better go quickly to see your God today because you have been spat out by the Chinese people."

We answered no word to the Guards because we believed that God controls the future and He would someday deliver all of us from their evil. Since we were not the first to suffer persecution for our faith, we found strength in remembering other suffering people of God. The Psalmist shouted, *"Many there be which say of my soul, There is no help for him in God. I will not be afraid of ten thousands of people, that have set themselves against me round about. Arise, O Lord; save me, O my God: for thou hast smitten all mine enemies upon the cheek bone; thou hast broken the teeth of the ungodly."* (Psalms 3:2, 6-7)

A Time of Chaos

The Cultural Revolution was a massive political movement – the proletarian class struggling against all nonproletarian elements. Actually, Mao was stirring up the proletarian class against his political rivals. It developed quickly with extreme savagery. Red Guards all over China shouted slogans, "Revolution is not like feasting or an invitation to dinner. Savagery is the way of a revolution." During these years there was no education, no normal work, no peace, no respect, no morality, and no honor. Instead of good deeds and virtues, there was only shouting, screaming, fighting, chaos, beatings, robberies, rapes, assaults, suicides, and murders. China was not a nation of human beings but a land possessed and controlled by the devil.

The youthful Guards established a "Red Guard's Headquarters" in our house. Up to twenty of them occupied our favorite rooms in which our family for years had shared pleasant times. They forced six of us to live in one small bedroom. It was bare except for two small wooden stools and two little chests for the few old clothes they let us keep. We slept on the wooden floor without a carpet or even a cushion.

One evening these crazed Guards caught two young people suspected of opposing their orders. They took the accused young men up to the third story of our house to a room that our parents had dedicated as a special place for prayer. The Guards were policemen, judge, and jury at that time. In this sacred place they beat their prisoners with fists, belts, and rods. They cut them with knives. Downstairs we heard the two men crying and shrieking through the night.

The Red Guards laughed loudly saying, "No beating, no confessing. We are owners of the country and we will beat you to death. " Then came the chilling sounds of more blows on bare flesh – thud... thud... thud!

At dawn the Guards ordered all of us to go upstairs to watch the penalty they gave to the two young men.

The Cultural Revolution Hits Home 25

We saw them kneeling naked and trembling on the floor. On their backs were bloody gashes from the knives and blue welts from the beatings. On the table was a bowl of salt water that the Guards rubbed into the bleeding wounds. The victims screamed with pain.

The Guards threatened us with similar punishment if we said one word against them or told anyone what they were doing. We longed to leave our house, but without their permission we could not. We were like sheep living among wolves.

During these days a young couple teaching German in one of the universities was forced to explain why they were not satisfied with the Cultural Revolution. They were then insulted and beaten repeatedly. Life became unbearable. One night, alone in their room, they used the lamp and two pieces of wood to form the shadow of a cross on the wall. This was their last Christian witness. In desperation, they hung themselves, one on each side of the cross.

Because of the overwhelming pressure of persecution, a young unmarried pianist living with her mother and younger brother, turned on the gas stove and took their lives.

Confucius taught the Chinese people, "There are three things of which the superior man stands in awe. He stands in awe of the ordinances of Heaven. He stands in awe of great men. He stands in awe of the words of sages." The Red Guards wanted to turn the people against this ancient cultural wisdom. In the fury of the times, teachers in schools, professors in universities, and respected elders everywhere were ordered to crawl on the ground with ropes, trash cans, or brooms tied around their necks. With these ropes the Guards dragged them from one place to another. They were forced to wear tall paper hats on their head with incriminating words. Passerby were invited to kick them, spit at them, or beat them.

A famous professor of pediatrics was charged with being an American spy. When he could no longer endure the suffering of being beaten with clubs and scorched with fire, he jumped from a high building and committed suicide.

An aged couple were beaten to death by Red Guards, not for personal charges, but because they suspected the couple's grown son, a world famous pianist, of opposing the government.

In the political persecution, the Red Guards were a law unto themselves; the police had no control over them. Theoretically the police could protect citizens if the Red Guards committed criminal acts, such as murder, rape, and robbery. But many times even these crimes went unreported and unpunished.

One winter night in 1967 three young Red Guards with cold weather masks on their faces boarded a public bus. They brought with them a young woman with her hands tied, a strong cotton handkerchief stuffed in her mouth, and a cold weather mask over her face. The girl could not make any sound, but tears were in her eyes. The bus driver asked where they were going. Professing to be her brothers, the Red Guards said they were taking her to a psychiatric hospital for treatment of a mental disease. Because these young men were armed with knives, other passengers dared not ask more.

No one questioned them although the girl bounced up and down groaning. Fortunately, the bus driver sensed that something was wrong, so he drove the bus to the police station nearby. Stopping quickly, he shouted to the passengers, "Grab the Guards! Rescue the girl!" With the testimony of the passengers and the threat of the police, the three Red Guards confessed that they intended to kill the girl after they had taken her to the suburb and raped her.

A factory in Shi Zhun province produced king-water, a mixture of nitric acid (3 parts) and hydrochloric acid (1 part) used as a strong solvent. The factory employed thousands of workers. Early in the Cultural Revolution, they split into two parties with different political views. At first the two groups only argued and quarreled. In time, they started fighting. First there were fist fights, then battles with self-made weapons – spikes, knives, and daggers. One afternoon guns and machine guns were smuggled in. Many died in the ensuing battle. Hundreds were caught and pushed into the sinks of king-water. Their bodies disintegrated without even a trace of bones remaining. Thousands died, tricked into mortal combat and cheated of life by nothing more important than a theory.

Desecration of tombs all over China was another of the disasters in 1967. Skulls and other bones were exposed on the ground. Dogs, cats, birds, and ants gathered around them. Thoughtless boys pulled these skeletons apart, kicking the skulls like soccer balls and playing among the bones around the tombs. Some took skulls and bones from the tombs home as souvenirs. China looked more like a nation of evil ghosts than a country of human beings.

An acquaintance told us that he had seen policemen shoot their prisoners and then eat the human brains with wine just after the men had died. I was sickened by these reports, but they were told with integrity. Also, citizens were asked to dig ditches and when they were done, the Red Guards told them to jump in. Then heaps of mud, dirt, and clay were piled on their bodies. These men and women were buried alive – the same way the German Nazis buried the Jews.

Tien An Mun Square in Peking commemorates Chinese heroes and reflects the achievements of the Chinese people. It is a huge square, beautiful and revered by all of China. On April 4, 1976, thousands of people gathered there in memory of their former premier, Chou-En-Lai. Jealous leaders of the Cultural Revolution secretly organized a massacre of these innocent people. Suddenly soldiers and policemen with knives and machine guns surrounded the square. No one could escape. They were not even allowed to surrender by holding their hands above their heads. Human blood flowed like a flooded stream, and corpses were piled high. Many of those who died had only come to the square out of curiosity.

The ruling leaders charged every dead man with a political crime: he was a "Reactionary Element." The families of these murdered victims had to keep silent. To speak out meant that one was branded as "a relative of the Reactionary Element." To be so charged put their lives in jeopardy.

These experiences might happen to one family, or in one factory, or in one square. But similar damage took place all over China in the time of Lin Piao, the vice-chairman from 1966 to 1972, and the days of the Gang of Four. The atrocities continued after the death of Lin Piao until 1976. Thus, the Chinese people lived with these agonies for ten to twelve years. Those who were scarred by the tragedies deserve our prayers.

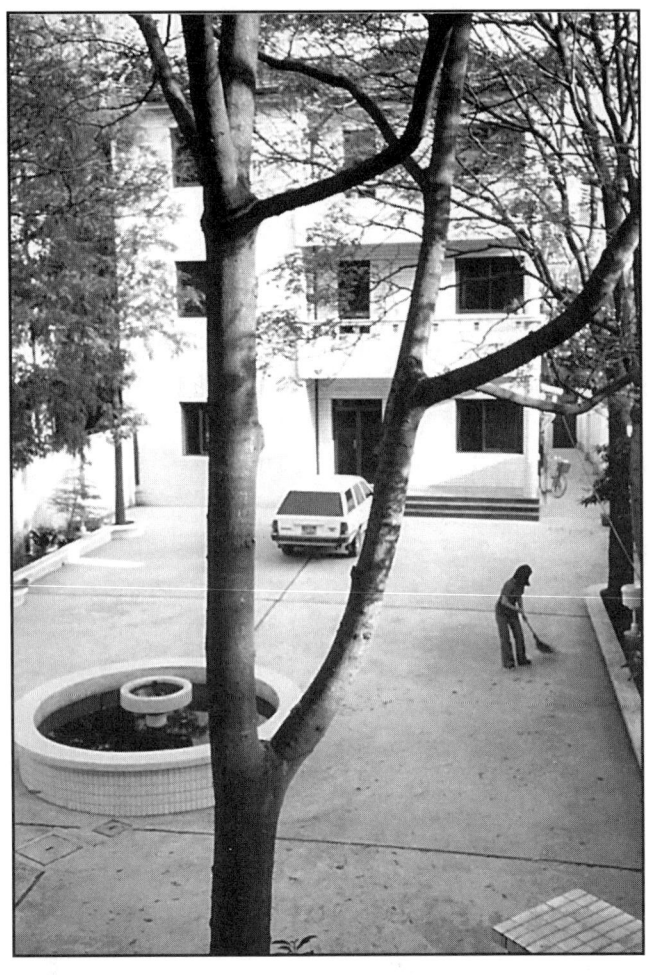

Our home in China before the Cultural Revolution

3

What Happened in My Family

Our situation was becoming darker, and life grew harder and harder. Nearly a year had passed since we had first been attacked. Everyone in the family had become political targets, therefore the Guards could do to any of us whatever they wished. My parents were forced to join other nonproletarian persons to sweep the streets and clean toilets and sewers under the supervision of the Red Guards.

One morning in November of 1967, all of the family had gone to work except my mother and a maid who worked in the home. Nearly thirty Red Guards attacked our home again. With unreasoning fury they beat my mother and the maid on their faces and heads.

As a result of her beating, my mother was admitted to the hospital for emergency surgery on her left eye. She stayed in the hospital for three weeks. Before her dismissal, we worried about her returning home. If she were beaten again before she recovered, she might lose the sight in her already injured eye. There was no place to appeal for justice. There was no law, no protection, no justice, no righteousness, no goodness, and no kindness in China.

In desperation, we asked God to help us. I went to all my close relatives and friends requesting that they take my mother in. Unfortunately, due to the political pressure, not even one person would open their doors to her. Then I wrote to a Christian young lady, Pearl, whom I had formerly known in our city. Six months earlier, she had moved to Guan Zhou to live with relatives there. In reply to our letter she had agreed to help. We then went to the police station to ask a favor. We asked permission for my mother and I to leave our home and go to a relative in Guan Zhou. Miraculously, the police gave permission for us to leave when my mother was discharged from the hospital. We felt glad for her sake but were sad to leave my father and other members of the family in the "mouth of the tiger."

None of us knew what would happen to us by tomorrow. Anxieties filled our minds. How could we live in another city without income? Could my aging father live through so many beatings? These were heavy burdens, but we thanked our Lord that mother could depart safely for another place where the Red Guards would not know us.

Because of our political status and for economic reasons, it was impossible to take a plane, so we took the train. Unfortunately, the jolting of the train so soon after mother's surgery injured her eye again, and she had to be admitted to the hospital for further surgery immediately upon arrival in Guan Zhou.

I repined at our fate and murmured about these further misfortunes.

I cried to God with tears, "What can I do?" Now I had the whole responsibility of care for my mother. How could I do it by myself? I was exhausted and sick of this kind of inhumane treatment.

I knew my own weakness and felt I could not suffer any more. Some Christians from this new city came to visit us while mother was in the hospital. They comforted and encouraged us. One good sister sent a precious verse, *"My son, give me thine heart, and let thine eyes observe my ways."* (Proverbs 23:26) I stayed with mother day and night in the hospital, relieved occasionally by others who came to visit us. Pearl came to the hospital nearly everyday to visit my mother and to help care for her. Her kind care and happy spirit were as refreshing as a drink of cool water. She did it freely. I could clearly see her love and her goodness. Gradually, I realized she was meant to be someone very special to me and to my family.

I had read in the Bible, *"And let it come to pass, that the damsel to whom I shall say, Let down thy pitcher, I pray thee, that I may drink; and she shall say, Drink, and I will give thy camels drink also: let the same be she that thou has appointed for thy servant Isaac; and thereby shall I know that thou hast shewed kindness unto my master."* (Genesis 24:14) This was the criterion of Abraham's servant looking for a wife for Isaac. This verse also became my criterion in looking for someone from God.

I wanted this loving helper for my wife, and she returned my love. When I asked her to marry me, she accepted, though we were both in the same oppressive situation. She asked nothing of me except that I bring a Christian faith to our marriage. By that time, we had both learned that material wealth could vanish in a moment. But we also knew that the words of God would last forever.

Her faith taught me that *"house and riches are the inheritance of fathers: and a prudent wife is from the Lord."* (Proverbs 19:14) Also God taught me that *"favor is deceitful, and beauty is vain: but a woman that feareth the Lord, she shall be praised."* (Proverbs 31:30) Thanks be to God for His good gift to me. We prayed together and then went to the official office to register for our marriage, planned for June 1, 1968.

Here let me testify from my experience. If you are wishing and searching for your beloved one, ask God to select the best one for you. Do not choose as worldly people do, asking for property, position, rank, and beauty. Pursuing these earthly values has destroyed many couples' lives and broken many families. We Christians should select from inside – the very inside. We need to ask, "Is there a firm spiritual base on which both are willing to build?" That Christian base comes from Matthew 7:24 in the New Testament. *"Whosoever heareth these sayings of mine and doeth them, I will liken him to a wise man, which built his house upon a rock."* Through the grace and mercy of God, I testify that we have had success in our marriage. We have been tested by many conditions, including prison life. We write these words wishing only to glorify God and to testify that God's Word is trustworthy. My wife, Pearl, never complained of our poverty or of imprisonment. She always cheered me up if there were any serious situations. She comforted me saying, "Don't worry; God has been helping us all the time. Let's pray and tomorrow things will be better." I thanked God for giving me such a good Christian wife.

My First Vision

The Bible tells us in the book of Joel, *"And it will come to pass afterward, that I will pour out my spirit upon all flesh; and your sons and your daughters shall prophesy, your old men shall dream dreams, your young men shall see visions."* (Joel 2:28)

What are these dreams and visions? Before I had this experience, I could understand very little. When I heard Christians talking about visions, I hoped that someday God would give one to me. But I also heard unbelievers talking about visions as one kind of illusion or a deceiving perception. Some would even say that a vision is the superstition of religion, including Christianity. At that time I could not refute an opponent, because I had not experienced such a communication from God.

Under special circumstances, or when some emergent thing is happening in history, God will show His order or His teaching by visions and dreams. Maybe the word should be capitalized as a proper noun. Such a Dream is no mere fiction of the mind unrelated to reality. I am a professional in the field of medicine, and I also work in the scientific area. My mind was very clear when I had these experiences. God gave them to me both in times of distress and in my happier days as well.

In the universe there is a magnetic field and an electronic field created by God. In these fields we discover truths that our physical eyes cannot see and our ears cannot hear. This is common scientific knowledge. From my experiences I believe there is also a spiritual field existing in the universe. As we give ourselves to a patient investigation of this area we learn more about the Spirit of God, the spirit of ourselves, and the spirit of evil in the world.

I hope more medical doctors and other scientists will research this field patiently and objectively. We believe that God is a holy revealing Spirit. If we humbly ask Him to direct us, He shows His power and His secrets. If you are an unbeliever, I encourage you to humble yourself. Ask God to save you from ignorance of His truth. As a medical colleague and a member of scientific community, I encourage you to explore the realm of the Holy Spirit.

Everywhere and anytime, one could hear the Red

Guards singing a song, which was very popular in China during the Cultural Revolution.

> *It is red in the East,*
> *The sun is rising.*
> *So rises Mao Tse-Tung*
> *Who seeks advantages*
> *For the people.*
> *He is a great savior*
> *Of the people.*

Tung means "the East." *Tse* means "to enrich." *Tse-Tung* means "to enrich the East." Mao is his family name. The Guards sang these words to praise Mao as a sun rising red in the East and enriching China. They praised him as a great savior of the people. Everyone, young and old, was expected to sing this song of praise to the leader. Everyone was to praise him and bow toward his picture before each meal. In a godless nation, this was developed from a form of emperor worship. But God reserves worship for Himself alone.

The Bible says of Jesus, *"This is the stone which was set at nought of you builders, which is become the head of the corner. Neither is there salvation in any other; for there is none other name under heaven given among men, whereby we must be saved."* (Acts 4:11-12) God's Word tells us that it is a sin to expect too much from any mere human being. There is no Savior in the world other than Jesus Christ. Only He can save His people from their sins. Only faith in Him and in His teachings can build a good society.

On August 5, 1968, my fiancée, Pearl, and I went out for some relaxation. It was a very hot day and I was tired. As we came back that afternoon on bus No. 25, I closed my eyes to have short rest. Suddenly I saw a vision. It was a big as a wide, light-blue movie screen. On it were red Chinese characters. The color was as red as blood.

    Frantic   Tung's
    Typhoon   Sides
            Falling Down

I knew clearly that "typhoon" meant a political hurricane – wild, strong, and terrible. I also understood that the "savior" who was making great mistakes now would go down and all who sided with him would also go down. This was my first experience to see a vision.

I told only Pearl and my mother about it, and we prayed that we might always be on God's side and in God's will. We knew that the message of the vision was in accord with God's Word. *"I have seen the wicked in great power, and spreading himself like a green bay tree. Yet he passed away, and lo, he was not: yea, I sought him, but he could not be found. But the salvation of the righteous is of the Lord: he is their strength in the time of trouble."* (Psalms 37:35-36; 39-40) At the time I did not know that the frantic typhoon would be blowing on us to the spilling of blood.

What Happened to My Family 39

The Chinese characters I saw in a vision. They were red on a light blue background.

Twelve years later in 1980, the public press in the United States verified the vision that God gave to me. I read these headlines: *"We Really Are Villains, Half of the Gang of Four Admits." "A Pragmatist, China's New Party Chief Has Been a Sharp Critic of Mao." "Mao's Widow Receives a 'Suspended Death Sentence.'" "Hua Resigns as Chinese Party Leader."* Today in 1997, God's vision to me has been proven accurate. From the time of the vision until today, I can witness through my thirty years of experience that the wisest action for anyone, whether rich or poor, laymen or expert, powerful or without power, young or old, is to obey God.

I am grateful that God showed me the future of my nation and the fate of those authorities when their power was at its peak. I could only kneel humbly in the presence of God and say: "How unworthy and low I am. You revealed this vision to me and made me understand that You are the only One who controls the heaven and the earth."

My Arrest

On August 31, 1968, we got an official paper from the government for marriage. We went to a restaurant with my mother and brother for a dinner of celebration. It was a very simple meal, and we were quiet but very happy. I felt sorry that our wedding day was so simple, but what more could I do? I decided

What Happened in My Family

later if there was a chance I would do more for my wife to compensate this valuable day.

On September 5, we went to the home of a relative for a visit. On the way, we had an interview at the government employment office and I was assigned to work as a doctor in a small hospital in that city. We then went to the housing agent and were assigned a permanent room for living.

When we arrived at my relative's home about five o'clock in the afternoon, he had no cheerful greeting for us. With a strained look on his face, he just said, "Come in. Sit down."

Before we could be seated, about twenty people along with a policeman from my hometown accompanied by several local Red Guards rushed in and surrounded me. They shouted, "Hands up. You are under arrest."

They bound me with rough ropes and cuffed my hands behind my back. They then took me out to the patio and ordered me to kneel down on the concrete. I demanded of them, "Why have you caught me as you would a criminal? I have not committed any crime. We have the official certificates from the police office to move here."

In reply they shouted, "You and your mother have planned to escape the supervision of the Red Guards. This is the most important law that you have broken. Tonight we shall put you in the prison because your arrest has been approved. Sign your name on this paper – the paper of your detention."

They continued, "There are many other crimes that we have found. You should confess. You must write down all that you have done." It came like a bolt of lightning. In front of them, I had no choice but to sign my name to the paper. My wife and I were then brought in a police car to a jail in Guang Zhou, the town to which we had just moved. There we were separated. I did not see her again for nearly three years.

As I entered the door, a guard ordered me to bend over, and he took everything I had in my pockets. After a little while he took off my handcuffs and ropes and led me to a room. It was early autumn and the weather was very warm. Twenty people were squeezed into that small room about 8 by 12 feet. It was now eight o'clock but I was not hungry. There was only a terrible thirst. I asked for a drink, but not one drop of water would be given. How could I bear it! I had never dreamed of being imprisoned, but here I was – without sympathy and with no valid reason for being there.

As I stepped through the heavy wooden door into that room dimly lit by a single five-watt bulb on a very high ceiling, I was stunned by the scene before me. The bare floor was covered with the sleeping, sweating forms of other prisoners. Along the wall, to my right, I saw a sink at nearly floor level that was used to collect human waste. It was carried out every morning and dumped by two prisoners. As the newest prisoner, my assigned place on the floor was beside the sink. I could not sleep. I thought of my wife whom I had just married and of my mother still suffering after her eye surgery. I thought of my own prospects. I could not pray; the turn of events was too sudden, too unbearable, and too painful. Tears came from eyes and sweat oozed from my skin making the floor wet. I could see nothing outside, except for two or three stars through a high window and a shaft of light through a peephole in the jail door.

Odorous the stink, hot the room, depressed the mind – and so many mosquitoes! It was the life of a prisoner that I was to experience for the next thirty-three months.

The next morning I was taken out for questioning. At that time, the police were also the lawyers because there was no law – only military rule. I was questioned three times during that week.

On the same day that I was taken into custody, my mother waited until eleven o'clock in the evening for Pearl and me to come home. She was worrying about us when suddenly she heard a heavy knocking. She opened the door and a crowd of nearly thirty Guards rushed in to search our room. They struck mother mercilessly on both ears. Then having finished their search, they left her alone in the room.

After one o'clock in the morning of the night I was arrested, the police released my wife. She rushed from the police station and caught a night bus home. When she reached our house about three o'oclock in the morning, she saw no light, so she quietly opened the door. Switching on the light, she saw mother slumped in a chair. The shocking events were too much for my mother to bear. Mercifully her sorrow was cushioned by a state of semiconsciousness. She struggled to regain consciousness. When she recognized my wife, mother began to cry. Quickly Pearl put her arms around her while she reported what had happened. They wept together with no one to comfort them. To cry was harmful for mother's recovery from eye surgery, but what else could she do? My wife knew that mother needed food, so she forced back her own tears and prepared food that they ate before they rested.

After I was put under arrest, Red Guards came every day to question Pearl and mother. My wife asked them for the money (500 yuan) I had carried in my pocket, but they refused to surrender it. At first they said, "There was no money in his pocket."

But my wife knew their plan was to keep the money for themselves, so she questioned them strongly. At last they said, "The money in the pocket of the Reactionary Element cannot be returned to you even though you are his wife. We assure you that he will be sentenced to at least fifteen years in prison. We will not press charges against you because you are so young. You were deceived by him and his family. You should reject him and all his relatives. We can cancel your marriage because you have had the official marriage paper for only five days. You can save yourself if you follow our instructions and tell us all that his family has done."

What Happened in My Family 45

To these words, my wife said nothing in reply. She knew they were trying to trick her.

The evening of the sixth day of our detention in the city, the police came to tell my wife that the next day I would be sent back to our native town and that my mother would be sent back within one week. Again the Guards pressed her to forsake and betray me.

I was handcuffed and taken to the railway station early the next morning. In the rail depot they ordered me to sit on the concrete floor, publicly exhibited to other passengers and workers in the station for ridicule. My wife came hoping to see me once again and to try to give me some clean clothes. But no way. She was told, "A young man with handcuffs has already gone."

She went back home with a heavy heart. But as she made the trip a song came to her mind:

> *Be not dismayed whatever betide;*
> *God will take care of you.*
> *Beneath His wings of love abide;*
> *God will take care of you.*

Again and again the words sang themselves in her spirit and with tears she was comforted. When she got home she told Mother, "I did not find him, but I have peace in my heart."

Right away my wife prepared the luggage for mother's departure. One week later mother began the trip alone by train to our family home. From that time, my wife Pearl had no further communication with my family. She began two years of life as a fugitive until she was captured and put into prison. During these years everyone in our family suffered bitterly, but thanks to our faithful God, His grace was sufficient for us.

We lived with the 23rd Psalm of David: *"The Lord is my Shepherd; I shall not want. He maketh me to lie down in green pastures: he leadeth me beside the still waters. He restoreth my soul: he leadeth me in the paths of righteousness for his name's sake. Yea, though I walk through the valley of the shadow of death, I will fear no evil: for thou art with me; thy rod and thy staff they comfort me. Thou preparest a table before me in the presence of mine enemies: thou anointest my head with oil; my cup runneth over. Surely goodness and mercy shall follow me all the days of my life; and I will dwell in the house of the Lord for ever."*

4

Life in Prison

After the journey by train to our native city Shanghai, I was ordered to sit handcuffed on the sidewalk outside the railway station. About midnight on September 16, 1968, a police jeep took me to prison where I would be held for the next thirty-three months.

In my prison cell, the walls were concrete, the floor was wood without carpet, the door was iron bars. There were three small windows near the ceiling, and no artificial light inside. There were no beds, chairs, tables, bathtubs, or showers and there was only one toilet. We were forced to sit and sleep on the floor.

The prison was built in a U shape, divided into sixteen rooms of different sizes. I was put in Room No. 11, about 12 by 24 feet, with around fifty other prisoners – persons guilty of murder, rape, assault, and robbery. It was dangerous to be confined with them, and I accepted a smaller food portion just to avoid their anger and mistreatment. Each of us had just enough space to lie on the floor. We were called by numbers instead of our names. My number was 1435. Our only possessions were the clothes we wore, a towel, and in winter a blanket that was shared with another prisoner.

We were not allowed to talk to each other, and no books could be taken inside except Mao's works. The guards argued that we could be truly reformed by studying the works of Mao. They tried to make us accept the idea that the words of great Mao could be "redemptive" to all who believe them. We were forced to read and memorize these writings. If we could not recite them, we were punished by other prisoners. I found that his words could not comfort my inner mind. I eagerly needed the Words of Life that had real power, not the words of knowledge or words of nonsense.

Those who memorized Mao's words did so just to show their captors that they were learning Mao's teaching. They wanted the guards to believe that their minds and thinking were being influenced by it. The truth was, the more they learned, the more skilled they became at convincing the guards of their conversion. They spoke whatever was expected of them, but in their inner minds they were unchanged.

By this strategy, they could be set free more quickly, but after several months they would be arrested and brought back because they had committed another offense against the criminal law. A young prisoner, about eighteen years old, told me one day privately that he had been in this jail several times. He said, "To learn Mao's words made me understand how to write and how to answer, so that I was released seven times."

Such behavior made me clearly comprehend that only Jesus can reform one's real inner mind to make him a good man. I know that God can save a man if he believes in Jesus Christ. But I have not seen strict laws, observance of the words of man, or punishment that would cause men to abandon their evil ways. I have also seen in America, a lot of criminals who after years of imprisonment, are released only to again commit more crimes. Human beings, the world over, have the same fallen nature and all are in need of the salvation that can only come through Jesus Christ.

Guidance From God

In prison, one day often seemed like a whole week to me. There was nothing of interest to challenge the mind. Only fear, uncertainty, discouragement, and great sorrow. We were not permitted to stand or lie down at will, only when ordered to do so. Police guards watched us scornfully. Because I was a political prisoner they paid close attention to my every act. We were forbidden to cry or show any evidence of our anguish or sorrow. I could only sob out my grievances to myself and shed my tears alone. No one was permitted to visit us or to communicate with us in any way.

I worried about my wife, my parents, my brothers

and sisters, my future, and even my life. The more I thought about it, the more frightened and confused I became. Some days I was nearly crazy. My brain could not be quiet, and I could not control my thoughts or my emotions. I felt that I was losing my mind, and I did not know how to prevent it. It seemed to me that I had lost my soul already. From my professional training, I knew I was going into prison psychosis and depression.

At that moment, God knew my weakness and my condition. He knew that I could not bear my burdens alone. Just in time, one night He showed me a vision. It was clear and powerful.

I saw a light pink curtain a short distance in front of me. It was drawn slowly across my area of vision from left to right. Immediately after the vision disappeared a strong voice came from above to my spirit, saying "See no one but Jesus only."

The vision and the voice awakened me and gave me great strength and peace of mind. I remembered the words of Paul, *"We are troubled on every side, yet not distressed; we are perplexed, but not in despair; Persecuted, but not forsaken; cast down, but not destroyed."* (II Corinthians 4:8-9)

From that moment on, I knew that I was not alone in the prison. Almighty God was with me and beside me. I heard His voice. I felt his presence. He was now teaching and protecting me. That was a spiritual sweetness as sweet as honey. I felt blessed and I could *"rejoice in God my Savior,"* even in prison.

From then on, I was able to shut out depressing and fearful thoughts about my family and the future. I could center my thoughts on Jesus only, and I began to recollect the Bible's teachings and its stories one by one. By humming remembered hymn tunes and recalling the words, I learned how to praise God in my darkest and most dangerous times. The Comforter taught me and cheered my heart through unceasing silent communication with Him. Happiness and deep inner comfort flowed through my spirit. Soon, my confused mind and vexed heart became quiet and calm. Sighing and sadness were replaced by praying and praising. I felt real joy.

The guards and some of the other prisoners watching my changing attitudes thought that I had no affection for my loved ones. They could not understand why I could be happy. The police often asked me, "Are you so cold hearted that you never think of the welfare of your wife, your parents, and yourself?"

I just looked at them and did not answer. But in my heart I knew I really loved my wife and my parents, even more than my own life. By God's teaching and by His love I had conquered the first big pain – sorrow and terror.

I wished that I could be free, but I had to obey God's command, "See no one but Jesus only." As a soldier of Jesus Christ on the battlefield fighting the devil, I knew that the most important attitude for me was to take up my cross and follow Him. He had said, *"He that loveth father or mother more than me is not worthy of me: and he that loveth son or daughter more than me is not worthy of me. And he that taketh not his cross, and followeth after me is not worthy of me."* (Matthew 10:37-38).

I always hummed this song when I felt timid and discouraged.

> *Onward Christian soldiers!*
> *Marching as to war,*
> *With the cross of Jesus,*
> *Going on before.*
> *Christ, the royal Master,*
> *Leads against the foe;*
> *Forward into battle,*
> *See, His banners go!*
> *Onward Christian soldiers!*
> *Marching as to war,*
> *With the cross of Jesus,*
> *Going on before.*
> –Sabrine Baring-Gould

Strengthened in Hunger

The Holy Spirit was teaching me that all we are and all we have has been given to us by God. We must, in turn, place these gifts at His disposal. When we do this, we need not fear whatever we have to meet. We may firmly trust, and rely on Him to lead us. He goes so far as to tell us: *"And fear not them which kill the body, but are not able to kill the soul: but rather fear him which is able to destroy both soul and body in hell."* (Matthew 10:28)

We were given food and water twice a day and a little drinking water. The portions were small and the food was of poor quality, hence the prisoners were soon near starvation. In spite of short rations we were given heavy work. We were assigned to tear off rubber from old rubberized fabrics. This recycled material was refined and used in a rubber factory. The fees paid for our labor went to the police.

The Red Guards had a motto: "Through labor you will be reformed. It is beneficial to every criminal. This is the only way to lead a man to be a good man." This hard physical and emotional pressure was applied to get the prisoners to confess to the crimes with which they had been charged. Often prisoners made false confessions to escape their anguish. They did not ask, "Is it right or wrong to make a false confession?" Under the pressure they only considered how quickly they could confess to a crime and ask for a lighter sentence. Also you could get the government's favor by reporting crimes of others – whether true or false. The prisoners often reported political misdeeds of neighbors, friends, and even relatives, thus many additional persons were put into prison.

In prison I saw a clear difference between believers

and unbelievers. Although very few unbelievers could bear the loss of material possessions, much less could they bear harm to their physical bodies. They were guided by Satan's philosophy: *"Skin for skin, yea, all that the man hath will he give for his life."* (Job 2:4) They would think up anything to preserve their bodies from pain – even if they surrendered their morality and lost their souls. To unbelievers the things that are seen and felt seem much more important than the things that are unseen. Almost no unbeliever could keep himself from surrendering to dishonesty when faced with starvation. For nearly three years in jail I watched thousands of prisoners come and go. Some were real criminals and some were political dissenters. I did not find anyone who could stand starvation except Christians who got strength from above.

I faced the same powerful temptation. After three months in prison I could not in myself stand firmly against hunger. I cried to God to save me from lying about myself or incriminating others. I asked Him to get me out of prison. He answered my prayer by giving me this word of strength: *"Man shall not live by bread alone, but by every word that proceedeth out of the mouth of God."* (Matthew 4:4)

I remembered that hunger was the first temptation that Jesus met. Until I myself was hungry, I could not understand why the devil first attacked Jesus with starvation. After forty days in the wilderness without food and water, the devil put on the pressure: *"If thou* be the Son of God, command that these stones be made bread." (Matthew 4:3)

I remembered that our Master had won out over this strong attack from the devil. Therefore I, as his disciple should learn from Him. I asked God to help me triumph over my desperate hunger. I repeated again and again the precious verse, *"Man shall not live by bread alone, but by every word that proceedeth out of the mouth of God."* Something wonderful happened. Though my body was still starving, I felt no severe hunger pain for nearly three years. I am positive that this was not psychological power, which might work for a few weeks or a few months. This was real spiritual power of His Words to hold my body and my life. Now I understand more clearly what Jesus meant: *"It is the spirit that quickeneth; the flesh profiteth nothing..."* (John 6:63)

The police often came and stood in front of the jail door observing me. I think they marveled at my body bearing up under starvation for such a long time. The prisoners commented to each other, "He was a doctor. Maybe he took good care of himself, or probably he ate especially nourishing food so he has been able to endure more than we."

In my own heart I thanked God for His power and for His Word. I could take no credit for my physical condition or for my peace of mind. I remembered what the Chinese philosopher Mencius said, "Thus when Heaven is about to confer a great office on any man, it first exercises his mind with suffering, and his sinews and bones with toil. It exposes his body to hunger and subjects him to extreme poverty. It confounds his understanding. By all these methods it stimulates his mind, hardens his nature, and makes up for his incompetences."

About this time I watched a Christian man who was in the same prison cell. I followed the practice of secretly thanking God for my food, but this man closed his eyes and prayed openly before every meal. Quickly other prisoners took note of it and to gain favor with the police, some of them reported the man's Christian practice to the guards. With permission from the guards, the prisoners began to beat him and often took away his meal. For the sake of praying openly he was willing to give up a whole day's ration. Like Daniel, this man never gave up praying publicly to avoid spying and persecution. When he missed his food for the day, he did not seem to feel hungry. It made the guards wonder about him.

In order to put more pressure on this Christian to stop his public mealtime prayers, the guards cuffed his hands so tightly behind his back that the pain could be endured for only a few minutes. He soon cried loudly, tears on his cheeks: "Lord, Savior, save me!"

The unbelievers laughed at him, but they watched his confidence and piety with much curiosity. I was not as courageous as he, but I sympathized with him and asked God to save this faithful Christian who glorified

Life in Prison 57

Him by accepting such punishment for his faith.

One day the guard came to the jail, called this man's number, and said loudly, "You are a simple and pure person, but foolish and stubborn. Now you are going to be released. Your mother is waiting for you outside the door. You should wake up from your superstition. How perfect you would be, if you did not believe in your Jesus."

The prisoners did not agree with the guards. They whispered cautiously to each other, "He really is a good man; he is like Jesus – so single-minded and steadfast."

I thanked God for his release, and for his good deeds. I praised God for our Lord's name being glorified by this man's courage and Christian witness. Punishment and starvation could not stop his relationship with Christ nor quiet his powerful testimony. Hallelujah!

When I watched him suffer so bitterly, I supposed that someday I also would be treated this way. "Can I stand as firmly as he does?" I asked myself. My answer was "No, not in my own strength." There was no man who does not love his own comfort. I thought of Simon Peter who tried to stand firmly by himself but three times denied Jesus instead of confessing Him boldly.

I could not imagine what I would do if put under such severe punishment. Would I deny Jesus, and betray those who were innocent? God forbid! I asked Christ to give me strength every day. If I should be confronted by a cross, I prayed, "Let me keep my soul clean, rather than surrender to the flesh or anything that belongs to it."

I sang a Chinese hymn for daily encouragement:
"Jesus, Jesus, don't forsake me.
Jesus, Jesus, You saved him
and I believe You will save me!"

More Severe Persecution

One night about three months after I was arrested, I heard a voice coming to my spirit asking me, "Do you love Me?"

I knew it was the voice of the Lord. Once He had asked Peter that same question. Now He was speaking to me.

At that time my spirit was full of sorrow. I knew there were times in my life when I had failed. Sometimes it was thoughtlessness or failure to pray. I cried bitterly, shedding uncontrolled tears. Shamefully and regretfully I replied, "Lord, I love you! Lord... Lord... I love You, but not enough... not enough... not enough!"

When I woke up my tears were still flowing and I was in great sadness. I thought, what was the use to offer Him more love here in the prison? Why had I not loved Him more before persecution came? There in the darkness, I rebuked myself for some time.

Who could know that the next morning I would be

called out for trial? God knew.

It was cloudy, cold, and windy. In a small dark room about twenty people stood around me. The door and the widows were shut and there was no artificial light. I wondered why so many people were there for the inquiry. One man asked me fiercely, "Will you be faithful to us?"

"I will," I answered.

Another said "If so tell us all you know."

I answered, I have committed no crime. I have already told you about my life and my work."

Before the answer was finished a policeman gave me heavy blows on both ears, and said. "We know that you are not willing to tell us how bad you are. But the facts are in the file. There is enough evidence to prove that you are an important member of the counter-revolutionary clique." Then they started to hit me with their fists and kick me from my head to my feet. It was very painful and I was numbed by their beating. One of them shouted loudly, "Shoot him! If you do not confess, double punishment will be given to you!" China's Constitution clearly stated that there shall be no beatings in prison. But the Red Guards broke the law easily and freely.

I answered nothing but simply committed my soul to God and endured all that I could. After a little while one said, "Do not fool with such an evil person. Cuff him."

Another spoke up, "Not answering will not

diminish your crimes. Your silence shows that you continue to stubbornly insist on your reactionary stand."

They then cuffed my hands behind my back tightly, saying, "We will not take off your iron cuffs until you reveal to us everything that you have done, and until you indict others for their crimes. You may be silent, but the cuffs will make you speak. Steel is more stubborn than you. Get back to jail and consider deeply your crimes. If you are willing to tell us the truth without reservation, our arms are outstretched to welcome you to the proletarian class. If you do not confess, you will receive punishment for what you have done against the Chinese people."

When I went back to jail, the guards warned all the prisoners, "This is a case of political crime. A bad man deserves his punishment because he is not willing to confess his evil doings."

The prisoners were surprised because we had lived together for three months and they had not seen in me any sign of anti-government activity.

When the next meal came, I was hungry. All day I had been without food and water. But how could I feed myself with my hands cuffed behind my back? Another prisoner saw my need and began to feed me with a spoon. When the guard saw him helping me, he shouted, "Stand up. Who told you to feed him? Are you siding with him against our government? If you feed him again, you will be handcuffed also. Let him do everything for himself. Let him eat like a dog."

The food was dumped on the dirty and dusty floor in front of me. I could only lick at it and smear my face, but I believed that God knew where I was and what I needed.

The handcuffs were made so that they tightened automatically if the hands moved, even a little bit. These handcuffs were imitated from the German Nazis and were used as a form of torture. After several hours, my shoulder joints and wrists became extremely painful. My hands were swollen until they could not move inside the steel cuffs and the cuffs began to dig under the skin. During the day the police forced me to sit upright in this painful position, rather than bending my back or lying on my side on the floor. The guard said, "This will give you a good taste of an iron fist. Why don't you surrender and confess? Remember the teaching of our Red Sun and of our Chairman Mao and Vice-Chairman Lin, 'Surrender your arms, or we will shoot.'"

But I had no firearms, no weapon at all, only a clear conscience and a will to do right. I did not agree to the Gang of Four and the Red Guards' destruction of China and her people. I wanted to be a good Christian.

That night, I could not sleep or turn my body. In the darkness I cried quietly, because showing emotion due to pain was forbidden in the prison. I shed my silent tears and prayed for God to deliver me from these evil men. I remembered that even the great prophet Elijah had requested that he might die. Was I stronger than he? No. So, I prayed with him, *"It is enough now, O Lord, take away my life."* (I Kings 19:4)

But a saving memory stirred in my mind. I recalled Christ's question to me only the night before, "Do you love Me?"

Only hours earlier, I had been awakened by my sorrowful confession, "I love You... but not enough... not enough... not enough." Then I pled, "God, give me strength to suffer all that is necessary, but command them to take off my cuffs."

The next day, I still had my hands cuffed behind my back. But the pain was eased when I remembered His love for me. I hummed a hymn that I had often sung without grasping the truth.

> *The cross that He gave may be heavy,*
> *But it never outweighs His grace.*
> *The storm that I feared may surround me,*
> *But it never excludes His face.*
> *The cross is not greater than His grace.*
> *The storm cannot hide His blessed face.*
> *I am satisfied to know*
> *That, with Jesus, here below*
> *I can conquer every foe.*
> *The thorns in my path are not sharper*
> *Than composed His crown for me.*
> *The cup that I drink, not more bitter*
> *Than He drank in Gethsemane.*
>
> Ballington Booth

Life in Prison   63

Without this ministry to my spirit I would have gone crazy. The pain was more than a human being could bear. Knowing the words of the Bible was one thing, but experiencing a cross of pain is very different.

For two days and nights I suffered. Then on the morning of the third day, the police called me out for inquiry again. They took off my cuffs, saying, "Have you tasted our iron fists long enough? Will you continue to resist? We hope you will be wiser now. You should know that we will be satisfied only if you confess all that you know. If you continue to refuse, we will cuff you again – this time for two weeks. Go back to jail, write down all your crimes!"

The judicial system in America is to find evidences for prosecution – "innocent until proven guilty." In China one was "guilty until proven innocent" which allowed the government to keep citizens in custody for up to thirty-three months.

I knew that I was falsely charged with crime. I could not confess an untruth and tell a lie even to escape further punishment. I committed myself to God and wrote the same true answers that I had given before. The police did not follow through on their threats, and I praised God for revealing Himself to me in time to give me the strength that I needed. I knew a deep sense of joy because He had given me the strength to resist this evil pressure. The power of His words was stronger than the iron chain. My soul rejoiced in God my Savior as He gave me a personal assurance of the reality to be found in Psalm 1:

"Blessed is the man that walketh not in the counsel of the ungodly, nor standeth in the way of sinners, nor sitteth in the seat of the scornful. But his delight is in the law of the Lord; and in his law doth he meditate day and night. And he shall be like a tree planted by the rivers of water, that bringeth forth his fruit in his season; his leaf also shall not wither, and whatsoever he doeth shall prosper... For the Lord knoweth the way of the righteous: but the way of the ungodly shall perish." (Psalm 1:1-3, 6)

5

Deepening Persecution

In prison, although I forced myself not to think of my wife, I always prayed for her peace and safety. I also asked God to bring us together again. I promised Him that if we could meet and live together, we would not live for ourselves, but only for Him.

A Sustaining Vision

One night I had another vision. I saw my wife wearing a dark red skirt with a white short-sleeved blouse. She was smiling and coming toward me through a wide gate in the garden wall. Over the gate I saw a large sign that said, "Village of Faith and Righteousness". Just in front of the gate was a beautiful flower bed with some boys and girls playing nearby. The air was quiet and I could almost smell the fragrance of the flowers. I watched her coming closer and closer. Then the vision faded. I awakened sad but also happy. I was sad to be shut up in the prison but happy because God had showed me that we would meet again in the "Village of Faith and Righteousness."

These two words, *faith* and *righteousness*, became my guiding lights while in prison. I understood as never before that I could not with my own mind and strength choose the words that I was to think, speak, or write. All must come from God. Without faith and righteousness, I could not trust Him for my life and my deliverance. The way of faith is narrow – but it leads to life.

"Now faith is the substance of things hoped for, the evidence of things not seen... But without faith, it is impossible to please him; for he that cometh to God must believe that he is, and that he is a rewarder of them that diligently seek him... Who through faith subdued kingdoms, wrought righteousness, obtained promises, stopped the mouths of lions, quenched the violence of fire, escaped the edge of the sword, out of weakness were made strong, waxed valiant in fight, turned to flight the armies of the aliens." (Hebrews 11:1, 6, 33-34)

I thank God that He occasionally gave me His vision and His voice to guide me while I was in the very pit. There was no one else to help me, not even a little bit. But the Holy Spirit is the Teacher whom Jesus sent. He taught me what I needed to know. Thanks be to God.

Do Not be Anxious

Jesus taught His disciples, *"But when they shall lead you, and deliver you up, take no thought beforehand what*

Deepening Persecution 67

ye shall speak, neither do ye premeditate: but whatsoever shall be given you in that hour, that speak ye: for it is not ye that speak, but the Holy Ghost." (Mark 13:11) This promise was often fulfilled literally for me in the prison.

At the time of Lin Piao, Mao's follower and Commander in Chief, they used a quotation from Mao, "Class struggle is the staff." The staff is the key link in any situation. They used this class struggle to stir up strife and fighting everywhere. Education stopped. Factories closed. Transportation shut down all over the country. Hospitals were closed. The only activity that never stopped was the class struggle – conflict over a social theory. There was no morality, no charity, no kindness, no love, no reality. It brought the country to the brink of total collapse.

The prisons were not immune from this social poison. The police said, "The prison is the focus of class struggle." So they forced everyone to accuse each other. They said, "It is the life of our party. If we stop the struggle, we will be killed by the bourgeois class. If you do not struggle against them, they will put us to death. You must follow Mao's teaching. Put it into action. Let us fight – struggle without stopping until victory is completely won in every field by the proletarian class. We must struggle not only to force everyone to conform but also to accept proletarian ideology."

Every prisoner was highly pressured to follow these

guidelines by accusing others – the more the better. In order to please the police and gain favor for themselves, most of the prisoners wrote down anything they had seen or heard from others.

Many innocent people were tortured, or put into prison. Accused prisoners were taken out for severe questioning and punishment. Under this system China's people came to fear and to hate each other.

One night I heard a voice in my spirit. It was a revelation from God to me. "This class struggle is self destructive. It can finally lead to death."

I understood that such immoral behavior was an evil next to death itself. I could not follow this path. If I did so, I would forfeit my morality and lose my soul.

When others followed the line, I kept silent. It thus appeared that I was against Lin's teaching – and it was a crime not to obey his word. They could charge me with a criminal offense and sentence me to death for it.

The basis of the Cultural Revolution was class struggle, but these theories and words were against God's truth. The communist government implanted deceit, corruption, hatred, and evil in the midst of the Chinese people as they taught the twisted words of Mao. Class struggle is self-destructive.

The classification of people with "class" led to the downfall of the Gang of Four. Later, when Lin Piao, the Commander in Chief, discovered that Chairman Mao was going to kill him, he tried to leave Mao's grasp, but his airplane was shot down by guided missiles. The class struggle caused Mao himself to die and Mao's wife and three officials of the Gang of Four to die in prison. After the death of Mao, class struggle was stopped. The classification of people with "class" was cancelled and no longer existed. Fortunately God taught me to keep calm and hide under His care. Thank God for His words of wisdom.

Forgive Your Enemies

In the face of this danger, Jesus' teachings were etched deeply into my spirit, *"For whosoever will save his life shall lose it: and whosoever will lose his life for my sake shall find it. For what is a man profited, if he shall gain the whole world, and lose his own soul? or what shall a man give in exchange for his soul?"* (Matthew 16:25-26)

The Holy Spirit helped me resolve to obey my Master's call rather than to follow the popular path. Praise the Lord, He led me in paths of peace!

What should I do when a close friend spoke words falsely against me for the sake of his own future? His accusations could sentence me to death. The Holy Spirit reminded me of the words of Jesus, *"But I say unto you, Love your enemies, bless them that curse you, do good to them that hate you, and pray for them which despitefully use you, and persecute you; that ye may be the children of your Father which is in heaven..."* (Matthew 5:44-45) Jesus also reminded me of His instructions to Peter in the Garden of Gethsemane, *"Put up thy sword..."* Sometimes I felt that humanly I had good reasons at least to defend myself, but Jesus said to me just as clearly as He said to Peter, *"Put up again thy sword unto his place..."* He helped me to obey His Word, although more often than not it seemed unreasonable to me.

I was convinced in my mind that His way was higher than my way, and His thinking was better than my thinking – but I could not feel it. The Holy Spirit really helped me to accept Jesus' way instead of following my own ideas. I was like a child obeying God's Word. Gradually He showed me that such careful obedience is the way we are to live in His Kingdom; it is the way we become like our Lord and Master. He took me through the *"valley of shadow of death."* By His help He enabled me to conquer my fear of the evils around me. He saved me from the stain of unchristian resentment and retaliation. But I confess, my most difficult spiritual lesson was learning not to fight back against persecution – the persecution that came to me because I could not take part in the destructive class struggle.

God seemed to vindicate me when suddenly the man who had lied against me lost his mind. All of his false accusations to the police were canceled because of his madness. Even until today, this person is still kept in a psychiatric hospital. He has been there for twenty-nine years. My prayer is that he will ask for God's forgiveness and God's eternal salvation.

Signs of the Last Days

The Bible gives some indications of the last days. The disciples asked, *"What shall be the sign of thy coming, and of the end of the world? And Jesus answered and said unto them, Take heed that no man deceive you. Then shall they deliver you up to be afflicted, and shall kill you: and ye shall be hated of all nations for my name's sake. And then shall many be offended, and shall betray one another, and shall hate one another. And because iniquity shall abound, the love of many shall wax cold. But he that shall endure unto the end, the same shall be saved."* (Matthew 24:3-4, 9-10, 12-13)

These words are an accurate description of what happened in China during the Cultural Revolution. Because men betrayed one another, they hated each other. This was a direct result of the following practices and teachings of the class struggle, which were couched in nice-sounding phrases to conceal the evil:

•Betraying one another was called, *"Helping you to realize your mistakes."*

•Encouraging children to rebel against their families was called, *"Saving parents from sliding into the deep pit of the bourgeois class."*

•Obeying the Red Guards' commands and all their orders was represented as, *"Loving and being faithful to your country."*

•Sacrificing yourself to provide luxury for leaders was represented as, *"Dedicating yourself to Communism."*

- For attractive young women to give their bodies to amuse or to be ravished by Red Guards in authority was called, *"Offering your youth for your motherland."*
- Persecuting someone more intensely was called, *"Liberating you from your bondage."*
- Doing more work for little or no payment was designated *"Serving your people."*

Such dishonesty is condemned by God's Word, which warns, *"Woe unto them that call evil good, and good evil; that put darkness for light, and light for darkness; that put bitter for sweet, and sweet for bitter!"* (Isaiah 5:20)

I have heard and seen many sweet sounding words, open offenses, bitter hearts, deceitful actions, shameful deeds, lips of trickery – with no real love. God is coming again soon. We must change our shameful ways.

Christians Who Suffered for Christ

In this ideological class struggle many preachers and Christian laymen were sentenced to long prison terms. Some were forced to work on labor farms. Others were shot. Churches were taken away and turned to other uses. They became secular meeting places, manufacturing plants, or cattle barns.

Due to illness a Christian pastor was released from prison to stay at home. One day a well acquainted Christian brother went to the pastor's house – begging for a place to hide. He told the pastor that he escaped from the Red Guards and they were hunting for him. The pastor sympathized with him but explained that he was also in the same situation. The pastor could not hide this Christian brother, but he gave him food coupons so that he could run away and have food to eat. Due to this, the pastor was shot publicly for helping a brother in Christ.

One Christian sister, just after the birth of her son was sentenced to prison for seven years because of her faith. When released from prison, she was not permitted to go back home, even though her father-in-law was dying of cancer. At her departure, her own parents cried but she consoled them through her tears, "Do not be dismayed or dejected. Every cup from above, even if bitter is also good. Christians should share Christ's pain and suffering as well as His grace and favor." After the downfall of the Gang of Four, she was vindicated by the police and permitted to return home.

Another Christian sister met similar persecution for the sake of Jesus. She, her parents, and her husband were all arrested on the same day. She was forced to renounce her family and was given hard work in the fields. One morning in the autumn as she swept up fallen leaves, she felt deeply depressed. Why had God done this to her and her family? Had they sinned against God? Were they worse than their evil oppressors? Was God just to do this to His children?

Through her tears, question after question tumbled from her tortured mind.

Under such oppression, China's Christians could only join with earlier children of God, saying, *"O God, why hast thou cast us off for ever? why doth thine anger smoke against the sheep of thy pasture? Remember thy congregation, which thou hast purchased of old; the rod of thine inheritance, which thou hast redeemed... O let not the oppressed return ashamed: let the poor and needy praise thy name. Arise, O God, plead thine own cause..."* (Psalm 74:1-2, 21-22)

Thank God, He hears the cry of His persecuted people. This Chinese child of God paused in her work and lifted her eyes to heaven for an answer. Suddenly she saw the heavens open and a voice came to her through the clouds, "Do not be in great sorrow, I am always with you."

She was greatly comforted and found strength to endure for more than ten years. Eventually, in 1979, her whole family was vindicated and released.

Our hearts can sing, *"Gracious is the Lord, and righteous; yea, our God is merciful. The Lord preserveth the simple: I was brought low, and he helped me. Return unto thy rest, O my soul; for the Lord hath dealt bountifully with thee. For thou hast delivered my soul from death, mine eyes from tears, and my feet from falling."* (Psalm 116:5-8)

A New Plot

Confucius said, "The progress of the superior man is upwards; the progress of the mean man is downwards." My captors, having failed in their rough and wild ways, thought up a tricky plot. Offering a beautiful girl to a hero or to a strong opponent is a famous plot in Chinese history. It is called the *Beautiful Girl Plot.* I did not know about the police plans, but the living and omniscient God knew them – and He prepared me.

One night after about six months in the prison, I was given another vision. A crowd of young ladies appeared before me; their arms were linked together, their heads and bodies swaying gracefully. They formed a half circle around me. At that moment, I heard a voice saying, "They behave this way, not to save you, but they want you to stay in the prison forever."

I marveled at this wisdom, but I could not understand what it meant or what would soon be happening to me. Early the next morning, March 8, 1969, the police came to the jail. they opened the door, called my prison number, and ordered me out. My hands were again cuffed behind my back and I was put into a jeep. As we drove, they told me nothing, but I feared I was being taken to be sentenced to many more years in prison – or even to be shot. All I could do was to ask God's mercy and deliverance.

After a ride of about fifteen minutes, the jeep stopped and I was led into a large building that I did not recognize. As we entered, they told me that this was a class struggle meeting. I must confess everything that they had charged me with and reveal everything I knew.

Again, class struggle! How obnoxious the words were to me! In the old dynasty, the authorities caught two slaves and gave them swords, put them in an arena, and forced them to fight each other until one was killed. If they did not want to fight, both would be put to death. On the stage the authorities drank wine and amused themselves watching the slaves kill each other. The time of slaves in China was long gone, but these authorities used other tortures in the 20th century.

The room was full of spectators. As I entered they began shouting, "Down with the rebel! Down with the running dog of the bourgeois class! Down with the children who cling to the bourgeois families! Long live the Cultural Revolution! Resistance leads only to death! We will not kill you if you surrender!"

My hands were cuffed behind my back, and the guards pushed my head and shoulders down close to the floor. Then they pulled my head up by my hair showing my face to the crowd.

"This is a good lesson to teach every one of you," they shouted. "He is rebellious against us. He must be sentenced if he does not change his stand today. Everyone here will bear testimony to his crime. Down with the crumbs of the bourgeois class. It is right to rebel against the bourgeois and their belongings. Making revolution is no crime."

I knew that I had not committed any crime against the law. On the contrary, they had broken the law by detaining me without a just cause. The power was in their hands temporarily, but I believed it would show the glory of God if I stood firmly. When I said nothing, it made them angry. Unknown to me, my brothers were being held in separate cells just off from this courtroom. At this point the police dragged them from their cells to confront me. The authorities intended to strike down our whole family, but God was on our side.

That morning they harassed and threatened all of us, but they could not get anything they wished to know from any of us. At the end of the morning I was warned that my attitude and behavior in the class struggle session was a crime. I was then dragged out in front of the spectators.

In the afternoon, they brought me into a smaller room on the second floor. They removed my handcuffs and ordered me to sit down at the head of a rectangular table. I wondered why the police had removed the cuffs when I had resisted them so steadfastly. For lunch they gave me a small amount of rice with a few bean sprouts – nothing else, not even a cup of water. They said, "We are giving you better lunch here than in the prison. You'll know how kind we have been to you." While I was eating, a number of young ladies came into the room – one by one. They all sat down around the table and smiled in a friendly manner. They inquired, "Have you finished your lunch? After lunch we will have a discussion. You may tell us what you learned from this morning's questioning."

I could not understand their behavior, smiling at me as if they were kind and friendly. In a low and gentle voice one of them pled with me, "You are the youngest one in your family. We wish to save you first and to help you out from the dirty pit of the bourgeois class. We want to save you and set you free, but only if you really change your stand and come over to our side. We welcome you to change. You are clever, because you have graduated from the university. We hope you will also be clever in politics."

Then another said, "It is pitiful to bury your whole life in the pit of the bourgeois class. We do not wish to punish you but to instruct and save you. If you tell us the things that you know without any reservations, it will show that you are deciding to break relations with the bourgeois class. If your testimony satisfies us, we promise to set you free after the meeting."

A third young woman picked up the appeal, "We know your whole family and your friends. We have not detained your parents, although they have a history of opposition to our proletarian class. Your parents and your wife are worrying about you. If you are set free this afternoon, you may go back immediately to be with your family."

The fourth girl concluded, "You were married only five days, were you not? We know how hard it must be for you to be in prison. Now is your best chance for release."

At that moment, I remembered the vision that God had given me the night before. I recognized that these young women were helping the police, trying to seduce me into saying what the police wanted me to confess. They would have succeeded if God in His providence had not forewarned me. He had told me clearly, "They behave this way, not to save you, but they want you to stay in the prison forever."

Months later after my release, my wife told me that at that time she was not at home. The girls knew that the authorities were searching for her to arrest her also. The girls were lying to me.

From this point on, I was respectful toward the young women – but unyielding. After two more hours of guile, they changed their attitudes. Pounding the table, they shouted wildly, "You stubborn fool! You are doomed to be sentenced! You should be shot! Put the cuffs on and get back to jail. You do not know what is good for you. Stay in the prison until you die. You are a rotten troublemaker to resist the control of the proletarian class. We should kill you!"

I now knew their undisguised attitudes and their real purpose. I stretched out my hands to be cuffed and went back to the jail knowing that they were very angry with me. I feared they would give me even greater punishment. I cried deeply in my heart, asking God to deliver me from their evil intention and power. As I prayed, a hymn came quietly but powerfully to my mind. I hummed the music again and again. My sadness and fright were gone. The words I recalled were:

> *Never a trial that He is not there,*
> *Never a burden that He doth not bear,*
> *Never a sorrow that He doth not share*
> *Moment by moment, I'm under His care.*
> *Moment by moment, I'm kept in His love.*
> *Moment by moment, I have life from above.*

With my fears gone, I remembered Jesus' Words, *"Blessed are the meek, for they shall inherit the earth."* (Matthew 5:5) Atrocity and ferocity cannot finally triumph, though temporarily they may be successful. I recalled the first vision that God gave me. I was sure that the vice-chairman, Lin Piao, the evil Gang of Four, and all who sided with them would eventually go down. The devil was temporarily frustrating God's purpose for my life, but I believed that God would use me someday as His witness and for His glory.

In our Christian walk, often *"we are troubled on every side, yet not distressed; we are perplexed, but not in despair; persecuted, but not forsaken; cast down, but not destroyed; always bearing about in the body the dying of the Lord Jesus, that the life also of Jesus might be made manifest in our body."* (II Corinthians 4:8-10) I thanked

Deepening Persecution

God for His Word that had lightened my pathway and guided me.

From a spiritual point of view, I realized that every evil thing that had happened to me was inspired by the devil, even though carried out by evil men. I knew this was a spiritual war against the devil, so I could not fight in my own wisdom or in my purely human way. If I did so, I would be defeated by Satan. There was only one way to overcome, by trusting and obeying Christ fully.

One precious verse of Scripture always admonished me on this point, *"Wherefore let him that thinketh he standeth take heed lest he fall."* (I Corinthians 10:12) The Bible teaches us, *"For though we walk in the flesh, we do not war after the flesh: (For the weapons of our warfare are not carnal, but mighty through God to the pulling down of strong holds;) Casting down imaginations, and every high thing that exalteth itself against the knowledge of God, and bringing into captivity every thought to the obedience of Christ."* (II Corinthians 10:3-5)

Here I want to encourage Christians in America who have freedom to do whatever one wishes, which is also a form of persecution used by the devil. I have seen many Christians suffering bitterly and trapped by the devil, who uses freedom to corrupt society with: 1) freedom of speech – to say whatever we please, to swear, to curse, to blaspheme, to judge, to gossip, to lie, and to condemn. 2) freedom of religion – to worship idols, UFO's, money, the devil, movie stars, musicians, and sports heroes. 3) freedom of sex – to sleep with many partners, to have orgies, to sleep with the same sex, to commit fornication, and to commit adultery. 4) freedom of press – adult video tapes, adult books and magazines, adult entertainment, sex "education," and pornography.

When I see this kind of spiritual torture, it is no better than being physically tortured in prison. I see the family structure deteriorating rapidly in the United States, so as Christian parents, I urge you to pray with your children and read the Bible with them daily. Go, as a family, to church every Lord's day for only God can guide people in the right direction and down the right path.

6

Ignored and Attacked Again

Something wonderful happened after this severe conflict and spiritual victory. I was held in the prison undisturbed for many months, except for being moved from cell No. 11 to cell No. 7, a room for political prisoners. There was no questioning. Everyday, I tried to follow the teaching, "See no one, but Jesus only." I prayed silently, hummed hymns very softly, and recalled the Bible verses that I could remember. At that time, I fully experienced that God's Word was my life. How hungry I was for His truth! How much I desired to have a Bible to read! Communication with God through prayer and singing hymns was my spiritual breath, but both had to be as silent as breathing.

Christians, please don't take your blessings for granted. If you have the freedom to pray, to sing hymns, to read the Bible, to worship at church – thank God for all these blessings and take advantage of these treasured fortunes.

A New Police Officer

Then one night I saw another vision. The frowning chief of police had on his winter cap. It was tilted to one side, and he was smoking. The white smoke rings showed clearly against the blue sky. As I was wondering what it meant, a voice said, "He is dry of plots and exhausted of wisdom."

I praised God for His revelation to me. Subsequent events proved the vision to be true. After several weeks, another young policeman about twenty-five years of age came to question me. He said, "From now on I am in charge of your case. The former officer has left for other work. I hope that you will be honest with me. I will not cuff you or beat you anymore. I wish you would cooperate with me so we can work out your case as quickly as possible. You have been under arrest for more than a year. Why do you admit your crimes only as slowly as squeezing toothpaste from a tube? The Chinese People's Government never wishes to destroy a criminal. We hope to help him improve. We try to encourage a good attitude toward us by your being honest and confessing quickly. But serious punishment will follow obstinate resistance. Do you understand our policy?"

I had never seen this young policeman before, and I did not know anything about his sincerity. But he sounded more reasonable than the former one and I liked his words, "I will not cuff you. I will not beat

Ignored and Attacked Again

you. I want you to cooperate with me to work out your case as quickly as possible."

Were these good words from his conscience or just from his lips? I did not know. The Chinese have proverbs saying, "Knowing one's face is different from knowing his heart." "You can draw a picture of a tiger's skin, but you cannot show his bones," and "A long trail tests the endurance of a horse, and time tests the heart of a person."

I did not know how to deal with him, so I breathed a prayer asking God to guide me and to protect me. Then I told him all the facts again. I concluded, "I have not committed any crime against the law."

One night a little later, God showed me a vision of this policeman. He was crouched low, sneaking like a thief through the gate of our jail yard. His cap was pulled down, covering nearly half of his face. After the vision disappeared, a voice spoke to my spirit, "Nothing can be found outside, now he is secretly searching to find proofs from your fellow prisoners for the charges against you."

Then I knew that this policeman was following the same plan as the former one. He had only changed his tactics with me. His goal was the same. The Gang of Four were throwing people into prison just to achieve their political goals. They wished to seize power, to change the government policies to satisfy their personal views. Political tests were made on suspected opponents, just as we had made chemical tests of inanimate materials in the science laboratory.

Persons suspected of divergent views were quickly arrested, tortured, and pressed to write down where they disagreed with the new policies. With those written statements in hand, the Red Guards could prove that their suspicions were true. With this evidence, they could send the victim to prison, thus sweeping away those who did not agree with their evil ways.

For fear of saying something that would be used against me, from that day on I scarcely said a word to the prisoners around me. After two months I was moved to cell No. 3, then in two more weeks, they sent me to cell No. 4, which was only about 7 by 10 feet in size. There were so many of us in a small room that we could hardly all sit down on the floor at the same time during the day, and there was barely room for us to lie on the floor at night. I could not sleep as well as some of the others because of poor health after being detained for nearly eighteen months. I was so emaciated that my bones showed prominently. I was short of breath because the room was too overcrowded and there was only one small window near the ceiling.

By the dim electric light through the steel grid door, I could see that there were hundreds of blood sucking bugs on the walls. All night, they crawled up and down. These bugs sucked blood from me and also from the other prisoners in the cell. From sucking all our blood, these bugs became big and fat.

One night I could not sleep. Thinking to help all of us by killing bugs, I swatted them against the wall. I killed at least 200 during the night, not thinking that they would leave bloody stains on the walls. The guards were terribly angry when they saw the stains. They were more concerned with the appearance of the walls than with the comfort of the men. One of the guards demanded angrily, "Why did you stain the walls with blood? Are you challenging us? You are to clean the walls and then stand erect all day until you recognize your fault."

Because of my poor health, my feet were swollen and my legs were so weak that I could hardly stand one hour. I did not understand what I had done wrong and why I was being punished so bitterly. But stand all day I must. It was an order and I was being punished. There were no basic human rights for prisoners at that time.

At one o'clock one afternoon, without warning, an accusation meeting was called in our prison. Two officers came to my room and ordered me to stand in front of all the other prisoners. Once again, the guards cuffed my hands behind me and pushed my head down. I thought it was an unauthorized cuffing by the local guards because I remembered the young police officer had promised me, "I will not cuff you. I will not beat you."

The head guard said, "We who have come today to conduct this meeting have never been here before. But this stubborn one has been standing against our government for a long time. He has not only done many evils outside the prison, but he has often broken the rules of the jail. He refuses to be instructed and reformed."

He then gave me such a heavy blow on my face that it staggered me. I saw lights flashing in my eyes and heard a loud buzzing in my ears. The guards then exclaimed, "How poisonous he is! To you prisoners he has the look of an intellectual, gentle and serious. But he is more poisonous than a viper. Do not be deceived by him. Think back and tell us all that he has done and spoken in this room. We already have proof of his crimes in our files. He stops at nothing. We will show all of you his final sentence." These same accusations and orders were given to the prisoners in all the cells where I had been held.

In order to please the guards, the prisoners one by one made charges against me. It lasted for five hours. My knees trembled partly from weakness but partly from fear because I was only human. I imagined that I would soon be sentenced – maybe shot.

At eight o'clock that evening, the head guard called me to his office and told me in a solemn voice, "We are always strict if you stick to your wrong point of view, but we welcome anyone who is willing to be converted. Now I am going to take off your cuffs and give you one more opportunity to repent. Go back to your room and write down what you should. We will not always be patiently waiting for your confession. You will be in contempt of our government and guilty of committing a crime if you continue to resist confessing your misdeeds. Your fate depends on your own attitude."

From being tightly bound for seven hours, my wrists were swollen and bloody when he took off the cuffs. I went back to my room and then reflected. Really, what crimes have I committed? They have ransacked our home and taken all our earthly possessions. They have taken me into custody and kept me in isolation cells. They have broken up our family; all of this they have done outside of the law. Why do they feel no shame for what they have done? They should confess their crimes for robbing us of basic human rights.

I still believed that truth would win out in the end. I could not follow their theory. I could not walk in the wrong path just because they had guns in their hands. Christ helped me to hold on to my faith. My spirit was strengthened when I recalled the testimony of the Psalmist:

"The Lord is my light and my salvation, whom shall I fear? the Lord is the strength of my life; of whom shall I be afraid? When the wicked, even mine enemies and my foes, came upon me to eat up my flesh, they stumbled and fell. Though an host should encamp against me, my heart shall not fear... Deliver me not over unto the will of mine enemies; for false witnesses are risen up against me, and such as breathe out cruelty. I had fainted, unless I had

believed to see the goodness of the Lord in the land of the living. Wait on the Lord: be of good courage, and he shall strengthen thine heart: wait, I say, on the Lord." (Psalm 27;1-3, 12-14)

I wrote not one dishonest word that the guards wished from me. The Chinese have a saying, "Taking away your life to get your money." It applied to my case at this time. I later learned that the accusation meeting in the jail was ordered by the young policeman to cover his dishonesty. When arrested, I had 500 yuan in my pocket. The money was put in the bag in my case file. This young police officer secretly took the money because he needed it for his marriage. To cover his theft, he decided to have me sentenced to fifteen years in the prison. But his charges were rejected by the high court for lack of proof, and he could not raise all of this money to replace it in the file. Hoping to get some significant proofs, he ordered the guards to hold the accusation meeting inside the prison – a thing that was almost never done.

Once again this young policeman demanded that the high court sentence me, this time for seven years. He based his accusations on the "proofs" submitted by the prisoners. Once again the charges were rejected by the court and the policeman was ordered to make certain of his evidence. It was God's blessed love and care that revealed to me the dishonest character of this policeman when He showed me the man in my vision as a thief coming through the gate of the jail yard.

Finally the young policeman took my cash and spent it for furniture, but no one knew it at the time because he was the officer in charge of my life. That much stolen money was not enough to satisfy him. Later he was caught stealing public money and was discharged by the police. He then confessed that he had already used up my money.

There is a Chinese proverb, "Evil is recompensed for evil, and good is recompensed for good. If not recompensed, it will be in time because when the time is up, all must be recompensed."

Caught Up Into Heaven

In April 1970, my wife was caught and put into the same prison. At that time I did not know about her harassment, flight, or imprisonment. If I had known about her arrest and being in the same prison, I could not have borne the mental anguish. God knew my weakness and He did not show it to me. It was His mercy!

From March of 1970 to March of 1971, I was imprisoned in cells 6, 5 and 9. They moved me from one room to another just to confuse my mind and to keep me from discovering their plans. The guards often put up new accusation boards with threatening words on the wall in front of me. One of them was, "Death shall follow after your stubbornness." Another was, "Bring your granite head to see your God."

Sitting silently from morning until night and sleeping on the hard wooden floor was cruel physical and mental punishment. From a little opening in my cell, I could see a few trees beginning to put forth their leaves. It was spring. Then summer passed. The leaves began to fall and it was now autumn. Cold weather set in. Winter had arrived again. It was time spent uselessly in such a place, with no hope, no value, and no future. I didn't know why I was alive.

I often asked myself, "What is my future? Can I ever be set free? Will the government shoot me or give me a serious sentence? How many years of my life will be spent in prison? Am I wrong not to defend myself when they accuse me?" The questions came because I was really weak in body and sometimes my faith faltered.

One night God showed me that one of my brothers was grumbling against me. He was saying that I should not have left home with my mother when I took her away for medical care. In my dreams, I cried out to him, "Knowing the whole course of events, you are grumbling against me, even under these conditions?" I wept under his criticism. How could he be angry at the unfortunate outcome of my efforts, instead of being compassionate and praying for me?

Later, after my release from prison, I confronted my brother and asked him, "Did you complain against me after I was arrested?" He frankly replied, "Yes, I was angry with you for leaving our native home. Then I

Ignored and Attacked Again 93

saw you in the class struggle meeting when we were forced to stand before the crowd and the accusers. Your face was pale and white as paper. I felt there was no hope for you to be set free. Because of your stand, these evil men were determined to put you under sentence. They were like roaring lions devastating and devouring our whole family." In that honest moment between brothers, love and forgiveness healed our wounds.

Some days in prison were especially filled with torment, uncertainty, and despair. I was often depressed and it was hard to get my spirit up. Special days in our family had come and gone – birthdays, wedding anniversaries, New Year's celebrations, and other holidays. These were days of bleak remembrance and dashed hopes. No letters could be mailed or received. I had not had a bath for a year and a half since I had been taken into custody, and I did not get to go outdoors except for questioning.

I told God that I could not wait any longer because I was sick. My body was beginning to swell and my belly was distended by fluids in the tissues. I could not stand because of weakness. I often sighed and, with Job, asked God impatiently, *"Wherefore do the wicked live, become old, yea, are mighty in power? Their seed is established in their sight with them, and their offspring before their eyes. Their houses are safe from fear, neither is the rod of God upon them. They spend their days in wealth..."* (Job 21:7-9,13)

I felt that my life would soon end. It was also the

time when my faith was tested to see whether I would be faithful to Christ even unto death. Many things I did not understand. But I knew that my Redeemer lived, and at the last He would take His stand on the earth.

During the time of my imprisonment, I was not always strong. Sometimes I was very weak in spirit. But when I saw Jesus, then I saw no one else – not my loved ones, nor the wicked; not even my very sick self. At those times I did not see the distresses around me. I would say to my sagging spirit, *"Why art thou cast down, O my soul? and why art thou disquieted within me? hope in God: for I shall yet praise him, who is the health of my countenance, and my God."* (Psalm 43:5)

I often hummed special hymns to clear my mind of fret, impatience, and despair.

> *All the way my Savior leads me,*
> *What have I to ask beside?*
> *Can I doubt His tender mercy,*
> *Who through life has been my Guide.*
> *Heavenly peace, divinest comfort,*
> *Here by faith in Him to dwell!*
> *For I know whate'er befall me,*
> *Jesus doeth all things well.*
> *-Fanny J. Crosby*

Another hymn also consoled me very often:

> *Jesus is all the world to me.*
> *My life, my joy, my all.*
> *He is my strength from day to day.*
> *Without Him I would fall.*
> *When I am sad, to Him I go.*
> *No other one can cheer me so.*
> *When I am sad, He makes me glad.*
> *He's my Friend.*
>
> - Will L. Thompson

Every once in a while, the guards would give us some sewing thread and needles to mend holes on sweaters, shirts, underwear, and socks. I didn't care one bit about sewing, so on the face of my small sewing bag, I made a cross with black and blue threads. It would be a good reminder for me to fight the devil even unto death. I recalled the Scripture, *"It is good that a man should both hope and quietly wait for the salvation of the Lord. It is good for a man that he bear the yoke in his youth. He sitteth alone and keepeth silence, because he hath borne it upon him."* (Lamentation 3:26-28) I tried to wait patiently for deliverance, because I knew that God's promise was to the one who endured to the end; he it was who should be saved.

One night I was caught up into heaven. I clearly knew that my body was still in the jail suffering bitterly, but my spirit, my inner self was in a very large and beautiful garden. It was clean and neat – not even a single leaf on the ground. The sunshine felt warm and comfortable. The sky was light blue and the garden was full of tall pine and evergreen trees. This was heaven. An old man, wearing a pure white robe, guided me through the garden showing me its beauty. I begged him, "Please let me stay here, just to lie under the trees. Even a small place here is better than suffering in the prison down on the earth."

The old man smiled and told me kindly, "No, you cannot stay here now. You will go back to your parents and serve them." Then I felt myself moving downward from above. I wakened from my vision with great comfort and peace. I felt a glow on my face, but there was no mirror in which I could see myself. The other prisoners commented, "His complexion is so good. Look! His face is bright! Why are you so happy today, Old Lagger?"

That was my nickname that they called me in the prison instead of using my prison number. I was "Old Lagger" because I was the one who had been in custody the longest – lagging behind, without a final sentence. They asked me, "Do you think the longer you stay in prison the happier you will be?"

I did not tell them what had happened to me. I just thanked God for His wonderful promise. From that day on, I knew for certain that I would be set free. This was about one year before I was released.

Pressures at Home

My mother had been ordered back to our native

Ignored and Attacked Again 97

town, and she went there by train two weeks after I had been arrested. She met my father at our house, which had become a ruin of brick and mud. Only the frame stood intact. But they grieved more because one of their sons was in the custody of the police and the other two were in segregated cells.

My mother and father could not live under the frightening circumstances. Only by the grace of God, were they able to go on from day to day. They were allowed only 10 yuan per month by the Red Guards. I thanked God that my parents, even in these difficult conditions, still tithed to help other Christians who were suffering more than themselves.

Although my parents were not put into prison, their hearts were broken. With their life savings gone and their youngest son arrested, they said that without Jesus they would have ended their own lives. Everyone would harass them. Even very young children mocked them. Most close relatives were far away and some reviled my parents. Former friends rejected them saying, "This is God's punishment and God's justice upon your household because of your sins."

One old Christian, however, gave my parents encouragement. When he was sick, God talked to him about my father and mother. After praying for them, he told his grandchildren, "This family is like Job's family. We must not despise them, even though so many people are speaking evil and slandering them. God will bless this family more and more. Go tell them of this promise, *"For he hath not despised nor abhorred the affliction of the afflicted; neither hath he hid his face from him; but when he cried unto him, he heard."* (Psalm 22:24)

My Mother's Prayer

One afternoon about the time that I got my promise for deliverance my mother knelt before God. She asked God to deliver me as He had delivered Daniel from the lions' den and saved Shadrach, Meshach, and Abednego from the fiery furnace. Interceding in the language of God's Word, she prayed, *"Can a woman forget her sucking child, that she should not have compassion on the son of her womb?"* (Isaiah 49:15). God answered her in the words of the prophet, *"Whereas thou hast been forsaken and hated, so that no man went through thee, I will make thee an eternal excellency, a joy of many generations... and thou shalt know that I, the Lord, am thy Savior and thy Redeemer, the mighty One of Jacob."* (Isaiah 60:15, 16b)

Mother was then led of the Holy Spirit to pray for more than two hours in the presence of God. Suddenly, a very peaceful and strong voice came to her spirit, "Shao Lin (my Chinese name) is my beloved. I am looking after him and I will send him back."

Tears of thanks and joy flowed like water, washing her wounded spirit. She praised God for His greatness and goodness. God turned her weeping into gladness and goodness. She happily told my family that I was going to come back. Praise God! We Christians have the blessed experience of being guided and inspired by the same Holy Spirit. Praise be to the Lord, who is living. He controls our destiny, our tomorrow and our entire future!

Dear Christian brothers and sisters, if you have any heavy troubles now, please use our experiences in the Lord and ask our true God for help. I assure you that He is living, He is with you, and He loves you.

In China three years after my release from prison. I had miraculously recovered my health, but I was in a state of depression due to the continued oppressive conditions.

7

Life in a Prison Hospital

At that time in China, an army substation came to hold supreme power in every important community. Even the police were required to obey the orders of the army. Several weeks after my vision of heaven, I felt led by the Holy Spirit to write a request to the representatives of the army telling them of my condition. I asked the guard for a pencil and paper, which were supplied immediately. They thought I was finally willing to write my surrender, confession, and conversion to their way of thinking.

In January of 1971, I was called out by three soldiers for an interview. Several times one of the three pushed my head with his two fingers saying, "What did you think in these days? Will you change or still be stubborn?" I answered nothing but told them that I was seriously sick because of the long detention, and I asked for medical treatment. After physical examination by two doctors, and after checking the blood and urine tests in a prisoners' hospital, I was admitted to this hospital where I stayed forty-four days.

I was put in a large ward with nearly fifty beds. How nice it was to have a bed again! I had not slept in one for more than two years. I was so weak and exhausted that when I got into bed I immediately fell sound asleep even though it was morning and the room was filled with medical officers and prisoners.

In the hospital I was given better food with three meals a day. However, in the ward we could not talk to each other or move about freely. The door was always locked. Generally, the treatment was better, but mentally it was nearly the same as in the prison. Every day we were required to read loudly *Mao's Quotations*.

This was my first experience in a hospital belonging to the prison system. We were required to attend indoctrination sessions called, "The Struggling Meetings." As prisoner-patients, we were forced to listen to indoctrination radio broadcasts. But even these contacts brought stimulation to my starved mind.

According to the theory of class struggle, every bad thought and deed was blamed on the bourgeois class. The Red Guards assigned the bad to the bourgeois class, but every good thing was credited to the proletarian class. Red Guards, however, found it difficult to explain why the children and grandchildren raised in pure proletarian families went wrong. A former political writer for Mao Tse-Tung was a pure descendant of the proletarian family. He had however, ordered 2,955 persons to be killed among 84,000 political defendants in Hu Pei province during the Cultural Revolution. These murderers were played up to be angels, and they made beautiful speeches. We prisoners were told that we should pay attention to them. That was only one case.

In the class struggle meetings, the teachers often dealt with men imprisoned for many years. Many of the prisoners had no interest in political propaganda. On the contrary, they wished to know about salvation in Jesus and the truths of God. I heard the head of the army personnel who resided in the prison say through a megaphone, "I wonder why these rotten troublemakers turn to searching for and believing God? Superstition! It really is unbelievable to me. Why? Why?"

He once asked a famous prisoner being sentenced for twenty-one years, a priest, to stand up and answer him. His answer was too soft for me to hear, but it was easy for me to understand. Everyone has a spirit that is inclined to find its true Creator.

I believe the searching for Jesus by prisoners was the sincerest and truest. They lost all hope in this world, but they did not give up their quest for the Creator. Dear friend, if you are still an unbeliever, I sincerely encourage you to find the TRUTH, the real Creator – and find Him now. Why not seek Jesus and take Him as your Savior today? I feel so blessed that I am able to tell you what I have learned concerning this fact: although people had lost all hope in this world, yet they did not give up seeking for their eternal salvation.

Do not wait until tomorrow. From my own experience I know that Christianity is no superstition. A human being always seeks after God, even if he is in total despair. We sometimes yearn for Him also in our hours of great pleasure. God is real. He will be easily found if you seek Him. He takes care of everyone who knows Him.

Attacked By Satan and A Light of Understanding

While in the prison hospital, I was first accused and then indicted by the devil. Satan is a spirit, but an evil spirit. He knows much more than anyone, except God Himself. Surely he is shrewd and more dangerous than any human being because of his long experience and power.

I assumed our thoughts came from our own minds. As human beings we have the power to solve problems and to plan how to take the next steps. I did not know that the original impulse came from the spirit world – either from God or from Satan. Now I know that our human brain has derived powers. If the original thinking comes from God, communicated by the Holy Spirit, the result is beautiful and complete. The Bible tells us, *"Every good gift and every perfect gift is from above, and cometh down from the Father of lights..."* (James 1:17) However, if the original thinking is from Satan, the result will be bad and destructive.

In some decisions, we just do what we think or

what we feel, but we should carefully examine every thought to determine if it comes from God or from the devil. From my experiences of failing God and also successfully following Him, I have learned that I do not have full control over my thinking. Even some scientific inventions have been given by God in moments of inspiration. I have read accounts of scientists testifying that their successful researches came from God. My own father gave God credit for an important personal discovery in his field of science. I have also had many experiences in treating difficult diseases for which God gave me the insight to heal.

Just as positive thoughts come from above, evil thoughts originate with Satan. Early one morning in the prisoners' hospital, as I awoke, a cruel voice came to my spirit from the left and below. The voice said, "You could be free and prosperous, and you could travel abroad, but only if you deny Jesus."

This voice nearly crushed my heart. My first fear was that the thought came from my own mind. Insinuating that the idea was my own, the devil made me afraid by reminding me of a serious truth, *"But whosoever shall deny Me before men, him will I also deny before my Father which is in heaven."* (Matthew 10:33) But I knew that I had never entertained such a thought, even for a little while. Sometimes it was dangerous to confess Christ, but I had determined I would lay down my life rather than dishonor Him.

I thanked God that He had given me

understanding immediately to know that this evil idea was from Satan. I recalled the third temptation that Jesus met. The devil asked our Lord to fall down and worship him. In exchange the devil promised Jesus all the kingdoms of the world and the glory of them. I thought that I was being tempted with the same appeal, but I knew that I should follow my Lord even to death and to firmly refuse the devil.

Then I prayed to God and asked Him to protect and save me with the blood of Jesus and His powerful Words, because in my own strength I could not win a battle with Satan. I then sang a Chinese Christian song, "To God I Must Say 'Yes', but To the Devil I Must Say 'No.'" I trembled with terror for a long time but gradually grew quieter. I felt that the demon had left me unwillingly, fearing the precious blood of Christ and His powerful name.

This is a precious experience for me to share with you, dear brothers and sisters. If you have an original thought, it is important to find out if this is from God or from the devil. If it is from God, we have to receive it, obey it, and follow it. If it is from the devil, we have to refuse it, not listen to it, and don't process the thought. If we do this, we cannot become a tool of evil and we will not disgrace God as a Christian.

There was a Christian brother, who suffered bitterly from cancer. He was a surgeon. He told friends that the Bible never had a verse that preached against committing suicide. He said, "If I can not bear the misery, I'd give myself a shot to finish my life." Some of his friends disagreed but some agreed with his thought. Personally, I began reading the Bible for God to give me His thinking. I came across Jesus' example when He suffered bitterly on the cross. He preached the Gospel to the last minute and won the victory. With God's Words, I concluded that this Christian brother was wrong and I prayed for him. With prayer, God would give this brother the strength to live on and to glorify His name. Amen. Amen.

God gives us the freedom to choose His way or to go the way of evil. So He sometimes allows Christians to meet these struggles, wishing to test us. If at that moment I had not recognized the voice, or if I had mistakenly followed its evil suggestion, I do not know what the result would have been. I might have gained success in the world, or I might have gone crazy. Thank God, I did not follow the evil voice, and I have been kept under His love and His care since then.

Satan the Deceiver

One Christian sister was punished almost beyond her endurance. She was forced to labor on a collective farm separated from her husband. Then the police lied to her and told her that her husband had been put in prison and would be sentenced soon because of his Christian faith. They also threatened her, "If you are still stubborn, your future will be the same as your husband's." She believed these words and lost all hope.

That night she climbed a very high hill with sharp rocks below. Standing there she heard a voice, "Why don't you finish your life tonight? What is the value for you to live in the world under such conditions? What is the hope for you to have a happy future? Maybe someday later you will also be put in prison. It is impossible to kill yourself there. Knowing the political situation, you had better finish yourself now. There is no hope, no future, no husband, no family – nothing at all to live for."

She did not realize that the voice came from the devil. She thought it was her own judgment – and it seemed completely right. She bit her finger and with her blood, drew the cross on her blouse. She prayed for forgiveness – and jumped. But God took care of His own although there seemed no way she could avoid death. There were serious skin and soft tissue injuries but no vital organs were damaged. She suffered bleeding and shock as a result of obeying the devil's words. But God loved her. He delivered her from death because she followed the devil's words unintentionally.

My wife experienced a similar temptation. One night as she was being chased by Red Guards, she went to a large well. The moon reflected bright and clear on the surface of the water. The night was quiet, and no one was with her. She was full of sadness and uncertainty. As she looked down into the well, it seemed the moon was smiling on her.

Life in a Prison Hospital 109

Suddenly a voice in her inner mind said to her, "You are despised by the country. You are useless for the future. You dare not leave for another place because you are being followed. Why not drop into the still water now? Just once and then all trouble will be gone forever. Just once. Just once. Just once."

She was unconsciously bending forward over the edge of the well. Suddenly an unseen Power pulled her back. She was like one who had been awakened from a dream. God saved her and preserved her life for His purpose and further work.

Such experiences remind us of God's Word, *"Neither give place to the devil."* (Ephesians 4:27) Paul encourages us, *"If we live in the Spirit, let us also walk in the Spirit."* (Galatians 5:25) Therefore, let us be careful how we walk. Let us draw close to Christ.

My friend, if you are thinking that Jesus does not care for you, you can be sure that these thoughts come from the devil. He wants your soul to perish forever. I earnestly admonish you to put away such thoughts. Plead the blood of Jesus. Ask our Savior to deliver you from the attacks of the devil. Christ alone can help, and He is ready to keep you by His power. He says, *"I am the way, the truth and the life."* Thank God He is!

A Revealing Vision

One night God wonderfully revealed to me a vision in the hospital. I was in a big two-story church worshiping and praising God with all foreigners around me. I did not get any word from God before the vision disappeared, so I just wondered about it and asked myself, "Is this a common dream?" No. I knew clearly the difference between a vision and an ordinary dream. Therefore, I kept it in my mind until I would know clearly the meaning.

Today I can testify that it was shown to me to prepare me for worshiping and serving in the church in America. Thank God for His revealing Spirit and for His loving guidance.

After this vision, I thought much about going out from my own land to fulfill God's will for me, but I was in prison. How could I ever do it? Sometimes I believed in the validity of my release, but sometimes I doubted and worried about the validity of these visions. I wished to see the proof of the visions that were not yet fulfilled.

Today I want to testify that all the visions given to me have been fulfilled. It clearly proves that God is a living God. He controls yesterday, today and tomorrow. Praise our mighty God!

8

Under House Arrest

After forty-four days in the prison hospital, I was discharged with the diagnosis of liver cirrhosis. Scar tissue had formed on the liver and it was hardening. According to my medical knowledge, I knew that the prognosis was very poor. The police sent me back to cell No. 9. I was extremely sick and my whole body was swollen. I was emaciated and weak, and my abdomen was so distended that I looked pregnant. There seemed to be no hope for me to be released, and with each passing day, I believed that I would die in the prison.

The guards wanted me to write words of gratitude to the police because of the medical care. It was hard for me to write such words sincerely, because I did not feel that it was a favor they had shown me. It was because of their cruelty that I had contracted the disease. So I did not write any word of thanks. Instead, I reminded them that it was their guilt that had caused my illness. Once again, they wished to soften my resistance, but I believed that medical care was one thing, but guilt was guilt.

They used all kinds of tricky language seeking to bend right and wrong to their own standards. But right is right and wrong is wrong. Jesus said the Christian is the light of the world and a saving salt in the earth. I felt that I could not follow their thinking and remain faithful to Christian standards of truth. In this tension, I identified with Paul when he wrote: *"As it is written, For thy sake we are killed all the day long; we are accounted as sheep for the slaughter. Nay, in all these things we are more than conquerors through him that loved us."* (Romans 8:36-37) I knew that God was with me, therefore I did not fear them anymore.

The guards were amazed at my attitude and could only reply, "We will give you the final conclusion as soon as possible. You will get your deserved punishment according to your bad reaction to us." But I knew that my destiny was in God's hand – not in theirs. And I was not fearful of their threats because I received the heavenly promise, "You will go back home."

One morning in May of 1971, a police officer about my own age came to the jail. Speaking to me in Mandarin, he said, "I will talk with you. Come out."

It was the first time in more than a year that anyone had talked to me about the charges against me. He led me into a special inquiry room and asked me to sit down opposite him. There were no handcuffs this time. Quietly and reasonably, he told me, "You have been detained for nearly three years. The government wants to resolve your case quickly. In all of my experience, no one has kept their secrets without confessing them in prison. You have been here a long time and your case is nearly finished, but some points are still not clear. You are sick, and we have concern for your body. Therefore, your case should be settled quickly."

I thanked God for these words and told the police officer with confidence, "Justice will win."

On May 15, 1971, right after lunch, a guard called my prison number and said, "Quickly, pack up all your things and bring them out."

Instantly a flood of murmurs broke the silence and depression of prison cell No. 9, "Old Lagger is going to be set free! Congratulations!"

Other murmurs, "No, it is impossible for him to be free. Only three days ago, the head of the guards shouted loudly in front of the door, 'You will get your deserved punishment, because of your bad reaction to us.' He is going to be sentenced."

I waved my hand to the prisoners, and many of them bid me a friendly good-bye. When I got to the front yard of the prison, the policeman who had talked to me earlier came toward me smiling, and said, "Today, I am going to send you home because you are severely ill. You may have medical treatment at home, but your every act still must be reported to us daily. Your case is not finished. You are still a prisoner, but a prisoner at home because of your disease."

The head of the guards and some others stood scowling and showed their unhappiness. They did not want to see me released. The policeman asked me, "Did you know that your wife had been captured and imprisoned?"

I answered, "No, I had not been told."

He said, "Her attitude was much better than yours. She has now been staying with her mother for more than a year."

My heart nearly burst with joy. I recollected the vision that God had showed me that we would meet together in the "Village of Faith and Righteousness." It seemed God's vision was to be fully accomplished. But the policeman cautioned me, "You cannot inform your wife that you have been sent home. You cannot contact her. You cannot do anything without our knowledge and consent. If you do, you will bear the full responsibility. We will continue to investigate your case. Now, sign your name on the back of your release papers."

Having signed the papers, I was led out of the jail. My father and brother had been informed and they waited outside to take me home. Because I was still a prisoner, we knew that we dared not show our emotions when we met. If we did, these guards could accuse us of another political crime. We all restrained our tears.

As we left the jail, some of the guards were watching us closely. I was very ill and my legs did not have much strength, so I had to walk slowly. A guard came up behind me and kicked my left leg, shouting, "Why do you walk so slowly? Be quick!"

I was nearly knocked down, but I understood that he was testing me to see if I was really sick. He was still not willing for me to be released.

When we got to the home of my parents, we hugged each other. But since we could trust no one – not our neighbors, friends, or even relatives, our tears of joy were shed silently and secretly. I was astonished at the way God had led me, and my heart was full of praises. We knelt down and thanked God for His protection and His deliverance. Quietly, we sang Psalm 23 together: *"...Yea, though I walk through the valley of the shadow of death, I will fear no evil, for Thou art with me, thy rod and thy staff, they comfort me..."*

My parents insisted that I go to bed immediately and remain there because my whole body was swollen. But in spite of my illness, I could only praise God. With the Psalmist, my spirit sang: *"I will praise thee with my whole heart: before the gods will I sing praise unto thee. I will worship toward thy holy temple, and praise thy name for thy lovingkindness and for thy truth... Though I walk in the midst of trouble, thou wilt revive me: thou shalt stretch forth thine hand against the wrath of mine enemies, and thy right hand shall save me. The Lord will perfect that which concerneth me: thy mercy, O Lord, endureth for ever: forsake not the works of thine own hands."* (Psalm 138:1-2,7-8)

How thankful and excited I was after thirty-three months of captivity to be back home. It was unbelievable. All things seemed new. It was as though I had been raised to life from the grave. Now I understood why Jesus did not go to cure Lazarus immediately, even though He knew that Lazarus was mortally ill. From my experience, I can see that He was waiting for the right time to show the greater glory of God to everyone. Even Mary and Martha did not fully believe that Jesus was able to raise their dead brother from his grave. Jesus' greater miracle showed His love and power to all the people staying with Mary and Martha. Then the glory of His name was spread abroad.

I prayed the following prayer: *O Lord, if You had taken all my troubles away at the time I was crying to You, I would not have recognized You so deeply. O Lord, if You had taken all my troubles away at the time I was crying to You, I would not have understood my fellow men when they are weak and heavily burdened. O Lord, if You had given me peace and comfort for all of my life, I would not have sympathy for others when they are in trouble.*

Our Chinese philosopher, Confucius said, "The determined scholar and the man of virtue will not seek to live at the expense of injuring their virtue. They will sacrifice their lives to completely preserve their virtue." And, "If a man can for one day subdue himself and return to propriety, all under heaven will ascribe perfect virtue to him." Sometimes if a man sacrifices himself for the truth, even to death, it is really worthwhile in the sight of God.

Under House Arrest

Soon after I came back, some neighbors still wished us to fall into the political pit once again. They rushed into my room shouting, "You are under house arrest. You are still a prisoner. Is this not true? Be honest or we will put you in prison again. You are under the supervision of the local street government office. You cannot go out freely. You cannot speak freely as we do. You cannot engage in your professional work. All you can do is cooking, washing, learning Mao's works, and confessing and writing down your crimes. How bad and stubborn you are!"

My heart was sad when I heard these words. I wondered why these people were so hostile. Why would they show no mercy even though I had done them no harm? Why would they show no mercy when I was so severely sick? Why would they show no mercy even though I was imprisoned for three years? The Bible answered my questions and I felt akin to the Psalmist: *"I was a reproach among all mine enemies, but especially among my neighbours, and a fear to mine acquaintance: they that did see me without fled from me. I am forgotten as a dead man out of mind: I am like a broken vessel. For I have heard the slander of many: fear was on every side: while they took counsel together against me, they devised to take away my life."* (Psalm 31:11-13)

But God used this experience to teach me faith and trust. The more bitter the taste I got from men, the sweeter the taste of the Word of God that He gave me. *"If the world hate you, ye know that it hated me before it hated you. If ye were of the world, the world would love his own: but because ye are not of the world, but I have chosen you out of the world, therefore, the world hateth you."* (John 15: 18-19)

Led By God's Vision

The fourth day after my return, a knock sounded at the front gate in the late afternoon. It was not as loud as when the Red Guards came. I thought that it must be some relative or a Christian friend, coming to visit us. When the door was opened, my wife was standing outside. She said, "Do not be afraid. I come here with permission from my local street political leader. I come to visit you."

My family replied with terror, "Timothy has been released for only three days. He was warned by the police that he could not contact you and that he could not meet you. If he even visited with you, he would be put into prison again for disobeying their command. Your coming shows that he has violated the law. Who told you that he had come home?"

My wife only smiled and said, "Why are you so afraid? I have permission to come here to visit all of you. God showed me a vision and urged me to come to your house."

My wife was led into the room where we were sitting. We were stunned when we saw her. No one could say a word, but our tears flowed as she began to tell us about her vision, that she had seen four days before.

She said, "I was alone in a small boat. The wind was blowing hard and the waves beat against me. I could not see the shore and began to worry about how I would get to land. Just at that moment, I saw a man at the other end of the boat. He picked up the oars and pulled on them three times. Like an arrow, the boat shot quickly across the water and touched the shore. I jumped out on the sand and saw a beautiful church with high steeples in front of me. It was a building that I had never seen before. The sounds of church bells and organ music attracted me. I started eagerly toward the door. Suddenly, I remembered that I had left something in the boat. As I turned to see if the boat was still there, I awakened."

Pearl's experience was not a dream. It was a vision, different from ordinary dreams. As she puzzled about what it meant, a voice in her spirit said, "Go to Timothy's parents' home and visit them."

She had never entertained such a thought before because of the serious political situation. She had been warned many times by the police not to visit my family, or she would be arrested again. At first she thought it better to be cautious and not go for the visit. But her spirit was really troubled until she obeyed the voice of the Holy Spirit. She prayed, "O God, if this is Your command, let me be successful when I ask my political leader in the street office."

She had then gone to the officer at once and asked if she could visit her husband's parents. The officer readily agreed, saying, "You may if you wish." Without delay, my wife took a pedicab to our house. The three strokes of the oars were just equal to the three days that I had been at home.

We came to understand why the police had warned me not to inform or to meet my wife. They wished to created conflict between our families and between the two of us. They still hoped that one family would betray the other family and help the government. If God had not shown my wife the vision, telling her to come to see us, probably someone would have told her family that I had come home and did not want her to know. A deep misunderstanding could have developed. When they had warned me not to see her, I thought I understood their evil motive, but I was helpless to resolve the dilemma. So were my parents and brothers. All of us were blocked by the political pressure. But the Almighty God, the omniscient and omnipotent One, full of mercy and grace, showed His love and favor to us. Thanks be to God!

We both felt that it was not right to separate wife and husband. My wife went back to her mother's home to pray about it. I remained at my parents' home for what medical care I could get. My parents and I each received only 15 yuan per month. There was no money to see a doctor, to go to the hospital for tests, or to buy nutritious food or medicine.

The police did nothing to care for me. They didn't even return the money that was in my pocket when I was arrested. Due to my sickness, I needed that money for treatment, medication, and nutrition. The police released me from the prison to die because the prison hospital, where I had stayed, told them that I could not live longer than two years. The cirrhosis of my liver was an irreversible disease.

I was very sick. My liver was enlarged and my whole body was swollen. The psychological environment was also bad for me. My family told me many disturbing things, which upset and angered me. I was told that many men were still being shot for opposing the government. Before these men were put to death, the police bound them from the neck to the feet, so that they could not shout or move. To warn the people, they put the victims on a truck and drove slowly through the streets to the place of execution. These public displays told the people that if they dared rebel against the Gang of Four, the same sentence would fall upon them. My family said to me, "Every day we worried about you because of these unlawful times. It is an especially dangerous time before the date set for a public trial."

The Deeds Of God

Some days, I felt more troubled than in the prison, because there they did not let me know anything. Disease, poverty, terror, and uncertainty made me once again lack courage. I did not have the faith to go forward. I knew that I was sinking into deep despair, but I was so weak that I could not fight it.

I was like an exhausted traveler under the burning desert sun. With my human mind, I thought and thought. I knew my health was deteriorating and that I was very sick. I often asked myself, "Why did God send me home to die?"

One night, about two weeks after I returned home, I heard a spiritual voice very profound and clear. This time, the voice was speaking in English and not Chinese. "Hold fast of Him and you will see the deeds of God."

The voice lifted me instantly from that deep pit of despair. I thanked God for His unceasing tender love to me even in those terrible hours when doubts had assailed me. I really could not understand why the King of heaven and earth took thought of me. I was not worthy of His care. Men forsook me but God received me. In my weakness I was strengthened again and again by His unspeakably great love.

I ignored the words of the prison hospital doctors, who had said that I could not live but two years longer. The words were a true medical prognosis, for I knew the severity of my disease. But I did not worry about it any longer. God gave me peace of mind because I knew that God would not forsake those who sought Him. I understood and resisted my human weaknesses, and I prayed earnestly that I might trust Him fully.

Day after day, I gradually recovered and became stronger. There was no money to see a doctor, so I used God's healing power and my own medical knowledge to take care of my body. The only medicine that I took were some herbs and vitamins, because there was no money for other medications. Even the police who came each month as part of their surveillance marveled that I was getting better. After one year, I was in completely good health. All the blood tests and lab work came out with negatives and normals.

After three months, my wife got permission from her local leader to move to my home. In our home, every morning, we knelt privately for at least one hour in the presence of God in prayer. From the devil, there came terrors and worrying, but through prayer, they were all driven away.

"Hold fast of Him and you will see the deeds of God." These words were a light to me through dark times and even today still give me strength. I believe that it is a sure word from God for everyone who is under trials. God is the same yesterday, today, and forever. He never changes.

My dear wife, Pearl, whose story you will read in Chapter 9.

9

Pearl – My Wife's Story

I too was born into a five-generation Christian family. As a child I went to church with my mother and older sisters and brothers. I learned to pray and to sing hymns in the church. It was a beautiful and reverent atmosphere. In childhood, as a good girl, I understood that I should be honest, faithful, good to others, sympathetic to the needy, and hard working. I came from a family who loved the arts, so as a young girl, I loved the piano. My mother was my first piano teacher and she taught me piano lessons with strict rules. I studied hard and got high grades in school, but I looked forward mostly to practicing the piano after school.

After I graduated from the Peking conservatory, majoring in piano, I performed as a concert pianist and began to know more about what life was like outside of Christian circles. I realized very clearly the difference between Christians and non-Christians. I saw many kinds of evil in the world and recognized that true goodness is totally contrary to evil. I saw more and more the two faces of human nature. There was a smiling face, but also there was the dark reflection of an evil heart.

I was appointed as a piano and accordion soloist in a musical band by Premier Zhou en Lai to perform for prominent government officers and foreign diplomats. I was nineteen years old at that time. They treated me very well, even though in 1962 that year was called "a great natural disaster all over China." It was the year to return all the money owed to the Soviet Union, because there was great failure in the relationship between the Soviet Union and Red China. This was caused by Chairman Mao Tse Tung. Due to the lack of food, millions of Chinese people died. Because of the famine, I saw many people that surrounded our party hall who had swollen legs and begged for food. They watched as we ate. Eventually, I learned of this famine that would last for the next three years. Because I played music for high officials, I never missed a meal.

One day, my political supervisor came to me and chatted with me in a friendly manner. He told me that the government planned to send me to the Soviet Union to learn music and that I could get a doctorate degree there. After that I would be the only one to play the piano internationally for China. He knew that I was a Christian and so he said, "As you know Communist China has never sent a Christian to the Soviet Union. You may keep your faith in your heart, but you don't need to fill out your religion on the application form."

When he handed me the application to study in the Soviet Union, I was so happy to hear I could get a higher degree in music. Then I could perform on the piano all over the world, and I would be a world famous pianist. But if I returned that application unsigned, that would mean I disobeyed orders and would be forced to resign. In China, if one resigned from a government appointed job, for the rest of his/her life there would be no other job in all of China. My heart beat rapidly for my future, but I had to erase my faith and my religion. On the application, the first step was to deny my blessed Savior. NO! I would rather stay with my God than to walk the way of the world.

Therefore, the next week, I returned my application form to my boss – telling him that I would not go. He received the paper and said nothing. After that, I experienced severe political pressure and I had no choice but to resign from my job. From that time on, there was no promotion, no performance, no political status, no salary, and no future for me. I often cried when I came home to Shanghai. What should I do? I would now be a parasite on my mother, brothers, and sisters – depending on them for a living.

I prayed to God that He would open the way for me. With God, all thing are possible was the only hope for my life. I applied for visitation rights to see my second sister in Hong Kong, but my applications were denied three times.

The period of the Gang of Four was a time of triumph for evil human minds. The spirit of the devil could be seen, and the hearts of the righteous were deeply grieved. No one could avoid the disasters that resulted – not even the Gang of Four and their colleagues could escape from their tragedies. All have been sentenced for their crimes by the national supreme court.

As told in my husband's story, following his arrest, the authorities required that I send his mother back to her hometown on September 19, 1968. Right after she left, I was admitted to the hospital for treatment because of extreme cruelty toward us. My health was seriously damaged; my heart beat was very rapid, and breathing became almost impossible. When I went to the hospital, I was alone and there was no one to sign admission papers for me. No one knew me, and I had only a little money in my pocket – not enough to pay the bill. I stayed in the hospital for two days, then had to leave for lack of money.

Looked Like A Widow

I went to a Christian sister's home. She comforted me and we prayed together. I wore all black clothing instead of my favorite colors. I looked like a widow – I felt like a widow – no smiling, no happiness, and no joy. The loss of my husband made me discouraged in spirit, and my body grew weaker. Some Christians and other friends wished to help me forget my sorrows, but how could I? The more they tried, the more bitter I felt. No one could console me. Nothing could satisfy me anymore. Like Job, I began to wish I had never been born. I could hardly praise God because my husband had been taken away only five days after our marriage. Depressed and full of sorrow, I longed for someone who could give me real help.

One day, I went to seek help from an older Christian sister. She had fasted and eaten only one meal each day and prayed for the Chinese church every day for more than ten years. When I saw her I burst into tears. She prayed earnestly with me and sang a Bible verse set to a Chinese tune, *"My son, give me thine heart, and let thine eyes observe my ways."* (Proverbs 23:26)

It was remarkable how this precious verse strengthened my weak spirit and made me glad. She showed me other Bible truths, *"Every way of a man is right in his own eyes: but the Lord pondereth the hearts. To do justice and judgment is more acceptable to the Lord than sacrifice."* (Proverbs 21:2-3) *"Fret not thyself because of evil men, neither be thou envious at the wicked; for there shall be no reward to the evil man; the candle of the wicked shall be put out."* (Proverbs 24:19-20)

With her spiritual help, I went home strengthened, but I asked myself many questions. They tumbled in rapid succession from my troubled mind. I could find no satisfying answers to any of them.

Could it be worse? Is my life as bitter as it can be? Is there any hope it will get better? Ever? Is there any possibility that my husband will come back, even though I was told he would be sentenced for at least fifteen years? What serious crime has he committed? Why did he never tell me before we decided to get married? Is he really a criminal? Where are my mother and family members? Where are my parents-in-law? Where is my husband and what is he doing?

Hunted by the Police

One day, I was invited to a park by some friends to cheer me up. They rented a boat and were rowing and singing. Their intentions were good but my heavy heart was not lifted. If it had fallen from the boat, it surely would have sunk to the bottom of the lake like a stone.

I had begun teaching some piano students in order to earn a little money for living. That afternoon, I was scheduled to go to a student's home to give him a lesson, so the boat ride was interrupted. The boat stopped at the dock and I joined the others getting off. Suddenly, I felt someone pulling me off balance. I stumbled and fell with my right arm in the water. The sleeve of my dress was soaked so that I could not go on to my student's home. Instead, I returned to the friend's house where I was living. While changing my dress, I learned that some policemen with more than twenty Red Guards were hiding around the student's home and waiting for me. Someone had betrayed my schedule to them. But it was not the time for me to be arrested. God helped me to escape that trap. From that day on, I was a hunted woman.

Running for My Life

Several weeks later, another Christian friend came secretly after dark to see me. She told me that nearly all of my acquaintances and friends had been approached by the police to learn my present address. Some were being held in detention because they would not speak. She advised me, "As far as I know, none of these friends have betrayed you, but you should leave this city as quickly as possible."

I said, "Where shall I go without a place to stay?"

She replied, "I have some friends in a small city not far from here. I will introduce you to them that you may stay in their house. But the first problem is to get you out of this city. We cannot help you because too many people know us, but I will try to work it out for you."

She left, but came back in about two hours, telling me that my picture, as a wanted criminal, was posted in nearly all the stations, docks, and airports. I was stunned. I had become a criminal and fugitive overnight. How could I deal with the disgrace and fear? I burst into uncontrollable tears. When I grew calmer, my friend recommended a young man about twenty-five years of age to help me.

"He is a truck driver for a factory. He can drive you out of the city to my friend's home. He is a friend of mine; a good man, but he is not yet a Christian. Go with him now without hesitation. He is waiting outside."

Before we left, the young man said to me, "Tell me the whole story. Let me understand you completely. If you are not a real criminal, I would like to help you even if I am put in prison for doing so."

I told him everything and he realized my innocence. He said, "Follow me. I must help you if I possibly can." I thanked God for sending him my way.

The next morning, we planned on leaving the city in his truck, though it would be dangerous for us. He hid me with the cargo in the trailer and drove alone in the cab. We had to pass through the city wall; that would be the most crucial moment. As we approached the gate, he saw many officers on duty. They were carefully inspecting all vehicles. Even the pedestrians were stopped and checked. How could we ever pass? When they came to our truck, they simply asked for his identification, and wonder of wonders, did not open the trailer! God was with us. Sometime later, we reached our destination. My new friend had proved to be entirely honest and trustworthy.

I was in a city that I did not know and I had no certificate of permission to be there. I was received in the house of friends whom I had never met before, even though it was extremely dangerous for them. If the Red Guards came some night to search the house, I would be found and handed over to the police.

The plan was for me to pretend to be a visitor in the city for several weeks. Every morning, I had to leave the house where I stayed, pretending to make a tour around the town. Some days, I borrowed a bike, riding through street after street without any destination. I stopped when I felt tired. When I was standing on a street corner to rest, I feared somebody would know me or doubt my story. Occasionally, I rode to the farms or to a suburb of the city alone in order to avoid the attention of others. I had no water, so when I grew thirsty I had to drink from nearby streams. There was no place to rest when I felt exhausted, except to sit on a stone or on the ground. I had no food except one or two pieces of candy that I carried in my pocket; no company, but the birds and wild rabbits. I wondered why I still lived in the world.

But God did not forsake me. One day when I was riding the bike, Psalm 23 came to my mind: *"The Lord is my shepherd; I shall not want. He maketh me to lie down in green pastures: he leadeth me beside the still waters. He restoreth my soul: he leadeth me in the paths of righteousness for his name's sake. Yea, though I walk through the valley of the shadow of death, I will fear no evil: for thou art with me; thy rod and thy staff they comfort me. Thou preparest a table before me in the presence of mine enemies: thou anointest my head with oil; my cup runneth over. Surely goodness and mercy shall follow me all the days of my life: and I will dwell in the house of the Lord for ever."* Again and again, the words flowed through my mind.

I rode out to the farm and sat down on the ground to argue with God. "O my Lord, I am being chastened fiercely, and I suffer more than any girl can bear. Am I stronger than other women? Why do You give me these verses? Is it really possible for me to have a table spread in the presence of my enemies?"

Then I grew calmer and reflected, "It is good enough if I am not captured, and it will be wonderful if my husband can be released." I could find no other meaning, but these verses brought me much peace. I could hardly understand myself, because I forgot that I was being hunted. I began to sing some hymns and to repeat Psalm 23 aloud. I was happy that day in my communion with God.

True Friends

Five of my friends, including the young man who helped me move, took turns on weekends coming down to see me and to take care of me. They moved me from one city to another and from one farmhouse to another. They supplied me with what money I needed to stay alive. At the time, I could not give them anything, but I prayed for them and began to introduce these friends to Jesus. I tried to explain to them why

Pearl – My Wife's Story

Christians suffer so much more than unbelievers. I said, "If I had not had these troubles I would not have met you and could not have told you the story of our Lord and Savior. God has let it be hard for me physically but it is good for you spiritually. I praise God for all of you."

I soon learned that the young man who had first helped me was a heavy smoker and drinker. He felt there was no justice and no righteousness at all in the world. He was understandably troubled because there seemed no way he could get rid of his frustrations except to drink large amounts of strong wine.

Having heard the message of salvation from me, he stopped drinking and began to read the Bible and to pray every day. His broken heart was comforted because he had found the fountain of Living Water. He accepted Jesus as his Savior, and the other four were greatly influenced by him. God really blessed him for his faith. Eventually, he was miraculously brought out from China and came to America where he built a good life for himself and his family.

We met him again when we came to America. At that time, he told me how he had lost his job as punishment for helping me. He had gone to the blood bank every month and sold 100 cc's of blood for 20 yuan, so that he could buy food. When I learned that, I was deeply touched and prayed that God would reward him both in body and spirit. *"Of a truth I perceive that God is no respecter of persons: but in every nation he that feareth him, and worketh righteousness, is accepted with him."* (Acts 10:34-35)

"In Dens and Caves of the Earth"

During those first days of my flight I stayed in any one home only a week or ten days because my friends could not tell their friends the real plight that I was in. On the farms I was bitten by mosquitoes, fleas, and other insects. In the poorest farmer's home there was no place for me to sleep except beside the pig pen. The odor and the snoring of the pigs were something I had never experienced before. In the daytime I usually moved about aimlessly. If it rained or thundered, I sat under a tree alone or crawled into a hole or cave. Sometimes at night I had no place to sleep except in a ditch or grove. Wind, rain, snow, and silence were my cruel and constant companions.

I always carried a small Bible with me, and often read Hebrews 11:36-38, *"And others had trial of cruel mockings and scourgings, yea, moreover of bonds and imprisonment: They were stoned, they were sawn asunder, were tempted, were slain with the sword: they wandered about in sheepskins and goatskins; being destitute, afflicted, tormented; (Of whom the world was not worthy:) they wandered in deserts, and in mountains, and in dens and caves of the earth."*

I could only cry to God asking for all of us His mercy and deliverance from our present hard circumstances. If I had not been a Christian, I would have killed myself. When my spirit was the lowest I usually asked God, "How many women in this world can bear such afflictions? How many men could bear such cruelty? You know I am weak both in body and in my spirit. Why do You allow all these things to happen to me? Death would be better than these pains. Why have You set me as an animal in the wilderness without a home or a room to live in?"

When I murmured, the Holy Spirit often reminded me of the Words of Jesus. *"The foxes have holes, and the birds of the air have nests; but the Son of man hath not where to lay his head."* (Matthew 8:20) He taught me that a Christian should learn how to suffer in the world as well as to enjoy the companionship of Jesus. We are His disciples, and we cannot be higher than our Lord. After these experiences I know how deeply Jesus loved me. He had sacrificed His life without complaint. Remembering Him, I repented for feeling sorry for myself. I resolved to be a faithful Christian publicly and privately. But I knew it would not be easy.

Twice I seriously contemplated suicide, but God saved me from death. One account has already been told by my husband – I felt a strong urge to throw myself into a well but God spared me. The second occurred one night when I was on a large passenger boat taking me from a city to another farm. I could not get to sleep. Some power not of my own will seemed to pull me out of my room to the deck of the boat. No one was with me. I stood at the rail and watched the water running swiftly around the boat.

Suddenly the thought entered my mind. Why continue to worry about my future? Why tolerate all of this depression? I need only to jump into the water to end this meaningless existence. All my trouble will be gone. This way is the easiest and the quickest. Why not do it now?

I knew that it was from the devil, but I could not get away from the impulse. The course seemed right under the circumstances – but I hesitated a few moments. My girlfriend awakened and saw that I was not in bed. She jumped up and ran out on the deck. When she saw me bent over and looking down into the water she shouted, "Pearl, what are you doing? Come back to your bed."

It seemed as if I had awakened from a bad dream. I trembled as I followed her back to our room. If she had come five minutes later, I would already have flung myself into the river. But God had arranged for her to call my name just in time to save me. Deliverance came from God.

From that day on, I began to be strengthened by God's Word. I asked Him to deliver me and to be my help always. The whole situation outside was getting worse, but my spirit was getting stronger and stronger.

Sometimes, I slipped into the city where I had lived, to try to find a place to sleep. One night the weather was so cold that I dared not to stay out in the

Pearl – My Wife's Story

woods or in a hole. I disguised myself with dark glasses and went into the city to ask a good sister to help me for the night. She invited me in, although she was afraid to do it. I asked her, "Are you worried for taking me as a guest?"

She answered kindly, "I never refuse anyone who comes to me in need. You have come here in need, and God knows it, so He will protect us. Come in. Have some food and get a good sleep tonight."

After I had eaten the best meal I had had in weeks, I quickly dropped off to sleep. But about nine o'clock in the evening, there was a big noise outside. Someone shouted, "If there is anyone in this area who does not have a citizen's certificate, he must come out and let us know! We are going to search every family and check every home!"

It was the Red Guards. Unfortunately, I was in my friend's home with a certificate that I could not show because I was a fugitive. If they found me, both she and I would be arrested. Instead of sleeping, we prayed for God to send His angel to surround our room and keep us safe. He responded to our earnest prayer. No one came to our room though there were many Red Guards searching every home. After they went away, we quietly praised God for His protection.

I was so tired that I went back to bed and fell asleep quickly. But this good Christian sister knelt beside my bed and prayed for me through the whole night. I felt her patting me and she gently stroked my back and hair. In Christ's name, she had compassion for me. I was deeply comforted by the sound sleep and by her tender love. I shall never forget that night in her home, because once again I had experienced that God was with me. He had not left me alone. He cared for me.

The next morning God's good sister sent me on my way with some food and some homemade candies. I did not know where to go, so I wandered back into the country where I had lived in the wild. I was a girl of twenty-five, pursued as a political criminal although I had never had a gun, had never hurt anyone, and had made no opposition to my government. I could not understand why I had been declared a criminal and why they had put such a crime on me. The Chinese have a proverb: "The king intends his minister to die; the minister cannot but die." I was a little person, and the authorities intended for me to die. The political crime claimed by them was put on me without proof.

I now lived as an animal. I feared the wilderness and the animals, but I feared those human animals more. How long could I live?

Arrested

Four of the friends who had been helping me were under arrest and in separate cells. They were accused of helping an enemy of the government. Only the young truck driver was now free to help me. We had agreed to meet one morning at eleven o'clock at the bus stop. I waited for him until one o'clock in the afternoon, but he did not come. I was sure something had happened to him because he had never been late before. He knew it was dangerous for me to stand in a public place for a long time. Just before I decided to leave, I saw him on a bus with a frown on his face. He motioned me to go farther away, then got off at the next stop and walked back to meet me. He quickly told me in a low voice that the police had questioned him about his contacts with me and about the anti-government activities they claimed that we had been engaged in.

"I was ordered to write information about you and all the others involved. My political leader ordered me to remain in the factory. I was not to leave without permission. But I slipped out to let you know that now I am also facing terrible danger. Probably, this is the last time we can meet. I will be punished if I return to work. I will not betray you, even if I am put in prison. So good-bye for now."

I saw him go for the last time and was worried about him. I was sure that I would be arrested soon because I could not continue my flight without the help he had been giving me.

On April 26, 1970, I was recognized by some spies when I came to a friend's house for help. They went to the police and told them where I was. The police waited outside my friend's home and caught me when I stepped out. I was taken to the police station and confronted by policemen, Red Guards, and those who had betrayed me. The police from my native city were also there. I was faced by the same policeman who had arrested my husband and had stolen our money for his personal use. The important officer of the present government smiled at me disdainfully, saying, "Where will you go now? You are in our hands. Though you had wings you could not fly from our snare. No tricky counter-revolutionist can escape from the hand of the Chinese people."

I just looked at him and said nothing. A woman bailiff searched my pockets and my whole body. I was told to sign my name on the back of the detention paper, then two bailiffs took me to the jail. I shed no tears because the well of my sorrow was nearly dried up from all I had suffered during the year and a half since my husband's arrest. I had lived a hard life in the desert, in ditches, in fields, and in underground concrete bomb shelters. Imprisonment was just another kind of bitterness to me. Anyway, I knew that whether I lived or died, I belonged to Christ. I prayed a simple prayer in the Words of the Scripture. *"I entreated thy favour with my whole heart: be merciful unto me according to thy Word."* (Psalm 119:58)

The police questioned me several times before I was returned to my husband's town. A woman and a young policeman took me back by train. Fortunately my hands were not cuffed, but the woman was cruel to me. When I closed my eyes because of fatigue, she pounded the table and shouted, "You reactionary element, we will kill you after you have arrived! You are prohibited from sleeping! Stay awake and consider what you should do next, rest continually or surrender completely."

I made no answer because I had already entrusted my life to God. I had decided to keep my soul pure from sin. Wonderfully, Jesus gave me peace – true peace – in my heart. I did not fear what they threatened and I did not resent what they said to me. I trusted that Christ would carry me safely through, no matter what evils came. A line of a precious song gave me courage. *"On Christ the solid rock, I stand; All other ground is sinking sand."*

I did not know what the next hour would bring me, but I looked to Jesus and learned to lean on His powerful arm.

The Prison

I was jailed in the same prison, cell No. 13, as my husband. Neither of us knew that the other was there. There were twelve other women in my room. All were guilty of crimes except two of us who were political prisoners. The room was small, about 14 by 10 feet. Each of us thus had a space on the floor about 6 feet long and 2 feet wide. There was no rest room, only a urine tub. Each woman was allowed one gallon of water for all purposes. In the room, there were no chairs, no table, and no bed. We were treated like animals. Really, the cows in the government-controlled commune and the horses in the military stables were treated better than the prisoners.

Our two meals a day were of very poor foods. I had seen pigs on the farms that fared better. Because of the foul food, I had no appetite. My cell mates wondered why I did not feel hungry. They wished to eat a part of my food, but eating other prisoner's food was prohibited. They said to me, "You are crazy. Do you wish to die?"

The guard warned me, "If you refuse to eat, we have the responsibility to force you. We will open your mouth and a insert a long feeding tube down to your stomach, or give you injections of glucose intravenously."

I was so upset that I replied, "This food is worse than you feed a pig. How can a human being eat it? If you expect us to eat it, you should eat some of it first."

The other prisoners thought the guard would punish me, but he did not. Instead, he opened the door and took me to his office. There he said to me, "This is a jail. We cannot treat you as a hospital treats a patient. But because of your poor health, we will allow you to use glucose powder."

Every day they sent me vitamins and glucose powder. I ate these instead of the filthy solid food. The guard told me they had not treated any other prisoner this way. I was amazed that they had been so lenient with me, but their reasons for being courteous were wicked. The police and the guards both used the soft approach toward me. They hoped that I would be persuaded to cooperate with them but I did not give them any statement they asked for.

The Prison Hospital

Due to a lack of nutrition and to emotional stress, my heart rate jumped up above 200 beats per minute. I was sent to the prison hospital six times for examination and finally was admitted as a patient. It was a large hospital completely inside the prison walls. Here I saw for the first time the cruel treatment of the prisoners. Many of these inmates had been here for at least five years and some had been sentenced for more than twenty years. Most of those who had been sentenced to more than ten years were political prisoners, including Protestant Christians and Catholics. I asked myself why these good people should have to suffer for so many years. They were not robbers or thieves, nor were they damaging public morals. They had committed no crimes against the law.

Near my bed were two good sisters from a Christian organization called "Little Flock." They had been sentenced to more than twenty years in prison. Their chest bones and spines were now deformed and protruding in front and back as a result of the long period of detention and punishments. They groaned from the pain, but no one was allowed to visit them. Some of the nurses mocked them, "Why does your

God not come to cure your diseases? You are evil doers. Be quiet!"

I recognized them because I had heard them preaching when I was a little girl. My heart ached for them but we were forbidden to talk to each other. I could only pray for them, asking God to release them quickly. I had been told that they had already served out their sentence. I wondered if God had allowed me to be imprisoned at this time so that I could testify that they were faithful unto death. After my release, I was told that both died in the prison under suspicious circumstances soon after the completion of their sentences. I am glad that God allowed me to see them face-to-face, so that I can be a true and faithful witness to record the final stories of these two Christian martyrs in the history of the Chinese church.

I stayed in the hospital for thirteen days, but my accelerated heartbeat continued without improvement. When they discharged me from the hospital and sent me back to jail, I could not walk. When they questioned me, I could not talk. I was in very bad physical shape, but I wanted to follow the good way of the saints who had gone before. I had determined to sacrifice my life if necessary to be faithful to Christ. God was true to His promise. *"...God is faithful, who will not suffer you to be tempted above that ye are able; but will with the temptation also make a way to escape, that ye may be able to bear it."* (I Corinthians 10:13)

House Arrest

Unexpectedly on August 1, 1970, the same young police officer who had stolen 500 yuan from my husband's file, told me to get my belongings ready to leave. I did not know where I was going, but thought I would be sentenced and then transferred to a different prison. I was so sick that I could not move, so several prisoners helped me pack my few possessions. Then I said, "I am ready."

The guard opened the door and the policeman helped me out to the front yard. There he said to me, "We are releasing you to go home today because of your sickness. It is our policy to be humane to every prisoner. Nevertheless, your case is far from finished. We hope you will believe the government and because of our fair treatment you will change your mind and help us win over your bourgeois family. Your husband stubbornly resists us. He has now been imprisoned for two years but he has not yet changed his reactionary stand. We wish you to write down all that he has talked to you about and tell us what he has done so that we may help him change his mind. Your oldest brother and your mother are waiting to pick you up."

I was very sick and my head was not clear, so I did not answer him. I was too weak to reply. A little later, I reflected on my experience and my recent release from prison. I had seen many prisoners who were more seriously ill than I. They were still held. Why had I been released? Why this more humane treatment for me? Was it a trick? I finally decided either they could not find a reason to detain me or they thought I was so near death that there was no point in keeping me. The guard opened the gate and my brother, who had come for me, hugged me and took me out.

I stayed at home under surveillance. The police and the Red Guards worked together, coming to my home often to ask questions. Among the police who came was the dishonest officer who had stolen my husband's money in order to pay for his wedding. Sometimes the police and guards were courteous. On other days, they were angry and ill tempered. No matter what their attitude, I tried to avoid trouble by remaining poised and courteous. I knew that my husband and I were innocent. God must be allowing these things to happen to us in order to purify us and to test our faith and our love for Him. I had abandoned myself to God's will, and I believed that He would take care of us.

Reunited With My Husband

From my experiences, I can testify that God is alive and God is love. If we believe in Him, He will care for us. Praise the Lord! Faith in God is not a superstition. God is faithful to His children, and they shine as lights in the dark world. We Chinese have a proverb, "Temporary winning or failing is due to out strength or weakness; permanent victory is due to the truth." Jesus is that Truth. By His powerful hand and sweet love, I was finally reunited with my husband.

After six months I determined to break the police order that forbade us to live together. I asked the political head on our block, "What law in the Chinese Constitution forbids husband and wife from living together?"

She was dazed by the appeal to truth, and answered, "There is no such law."

Then I asked, "Since there is no law against it, may I move to my husband's home? He is sick and I can help him."

The officer was silent for a moment, then she said, "Since you are determined to go, you have my permission."

That evening I went to my husband's home and I remained with him. I had no work except caring for him and for our one small room. We prayed together every morning, asking God for His continued protection because there were still many people being sentenced publicly and put into prisons. We asked God to show His power once again and for His name's sake to move the police to release us. We were both greatly helped by the promise God had given to my husband. "Hold fast of Him and you will see the deeds of God." These words encouraged us when we were afraid and strengthened us when we were weak.

Both of us were usually self-reliant. We disliked being dependent. After I grew stronger, I especially felt ashamed to be supported by others. We wished to live alone, and we wished to work so that we could support ourselves. This desire is normally right and good, but God permited circumstances that made us depend on Him and others. He required us to surrender all our mind, will, and strength to Him in order to learn. It might seem easy to learn such a lesson in the home of one's family, but it was hard for us.

I was able to help my husband with his recovery from cirrhosis of the liver. I was amazed at my husband's miraculous recovery and we thanked God for every bit of His help and blessing.

10

Eight Years of Political Discrimination

On May 14, 1972, a policeman came to our home ordering us to go to the police station for the final decision of our cases. We reported there at eight o'clock the next morning. The police declared us free, from their point of view, without any further punishment: "From today your cases are finished. We have researched all the doubtful points of your family. We have not found any crime against the law. You are both free from house arrest." They continued with their usual lies, "You may live wherever you wish, and you may travel wherever you like. You may do and speak whatever you want." They then warned us, "You may not leave the way of our proletarian society and the thinking of Mao. If you leave, you will be guilty of a crime, and you will be put into the prison once again.

"Remember that both of you come from the bourgeois class. Because of this, your thinking is far from that of the proletariat. If you do not change to the proletarian stand, you will probably return to captivity.

Your minds are non-proletarian, and you have committed serious political mistakes, such as seeking more knowledge and living for yourselves rather than for the Chinese people.

"You also admire the new achievements of Western countries, wishing to learn from America and Japan, and you plan to leave your motherland. These are superstitions of your whole family. We do not care about your parents' superstitions because they are old and will have little effect on our society. But you are young. We cannot allow you to spread those superstitions and influence our newborn socialistic generations.

"The final decision for the both of you is: We can find no evidence of crime against either of you, but the husband has committed a very serious political mistake in his mind and the wife follows him. It was right for us to put both of you in custody. Do you agree with our decision? If so, sign both of your names on this paper of declaration."

Because of the political pressure, we had no other choice. We signed our names and accepted our release. They were always right and we were always wrong. That was the logic of those dark times.

We did wish to learn more of the sciences and arts in order to serve our society that much better. Great inventions were coming from the learning and research of other countries. We admired their efforts and wanted to learn from them. We could not follow these desires without getting into deeper trouble. If one sought learning, the Red Guards immediately gave you a "cap" to wear – a political label: rightist, pro-Western, traitor, reactionary, a man with a serious political blunder.

Because leaders of the Cultural Revolution feared educated people, they sent them to do manual labor on farms. Their slogans were, "Labor is the greatest blessing in the world." "Labor will purify everyone who has fallen into the muddy ditch of the bourgeois class." Also "Labor can reform one's mind to think like the working class, the peasant, and the soldier."

Another political term was, "grasping your queue." It meant that the authorities were watching everyone's acts and words – grasping at anything that seemed suspicious. These political devices and oppressive measures made the people in the whole nation frightened and miserable. In their opposition to believe in Jesus, those leaders were really ignorant of God's works and of His love. They had no reason to say any word against the Christian faith except that Christ calls for truth and righteousness. Also Christ calls for our supreme loyalty. We believed in Jesus, not only because we had learned about Him from the Bible, but also because we had personally experienced His reality. We could not deny what we knew.

We were aware that the authorities had put a political "cap" on my head. According to them, I was one who "had made a serious political blunder."

Because the "cap" was on my head, it was also on my wife's head. We both had political stains in our personal affairs files. We left the police board partly with a sense of joy and partly with a sense of futility. Walking home, I said to my wife, "We should praise God because He has spared our lives. Now our house arrest is over, and we may be able to find jobs for our living. There are still some problems, but God has taught us, 'Hold fast of Him and you will see the deeds of God.'"

We thanked God that He had answered our prayer. The authorities had released us, and we were together. What a good result we got from God through our faith and obedience. God's promise had been fulfilled – "You may go back home in the village of faith and righteousness." Our health had been completely recovered through God's power and His promise.

After twenty-seven years, while we are writing this book, we can see clearly that China has changed a great deal. This change has proven that those authorities during the Cultural Revolution were wrong in that they committed evil throughout China. Yet we Christians are right, because we follow an unchanging Lord, Jesus Christ, Who seeks to do good to all mankind. We cannot hate those who persecute us; we must pray for them to get out of the grasp of the devil. They need to know God and get His blessings and salvation too.

A Reunited Family

Before we were released, we had no regular living

space assigned to us because we were legally outlawed. We dared not even ask the housing board for a single room. Now that we were freed, we went to the leader of the housing board and asked him to give us back a room of the house that my parents had built. Several of the rooms had been closed by the authorities when the property had been confiscated by the government, and we thought it only fair and right to ask for at least one room as our home.

But the leader angrily challenged my wife, "Who told you to follow your husband who wears the 'cap' of serious political blundering? It was your choice. Now we cannot give you such a nice room for your home. This house now belongs to us, the Chinese people. If you had married a high government official, or a soldier, we could give you a beautiful apartment. Do you know the Chinese proverb, 'Follow a chicken if you marry a chicken, and follow a dog if you marry a dog?' You cannot live in this district because it is now reserved for high government officials. Your husband and you are both politically suspicious and unstable elements. We cannot allow you to live in this district – a political red zone. We shall give you a room in a district of the working class; there you will learn the good qualities of working people."

We were hurt by the insults and the arrogance of their political discrimination, but as Christians we are asked to follow Jesus in this world, no matter how poor or how difficult the circumstances. We had no choice.

We moved to the room assigned to us and lived there in the slum quarters for seven and a half years. The room was small, without a toilet or bath. We shared a common kitchen with three other families. It was crowded but we got along quite well.

Although this was a kind of political pressure, it was much better than life in the prison. There was no comparison to our previous lives. We learned an important lesson that Christians should stand firm and have joy in the Lord no matter what circumstances we encounter. As Job (1:21) in the Bible praised God through the good and the bad times, so must we. *"...the Lord gave, and the Lord hath taken away; blessed be the name of the Lord."* Our only goal is to serve our Master who loved us and died for us.

Under Economic Discrimination

To earn a living, I now had to find some kind of job. Fortunately, the authorities recognized my medical training and gave me a job as a doctor in a district community hospital. But because of my prison record, they did not give me the salary I had been earning before I was arrested. I received only 43 yuan a month, which was equivalent to about ten U.S. dollars. For this I worked six days each week. That equaled about seventeen cents in U.S. money each day for two people – rent, utility, gas, water, clothing, food, everything.

Under political discrimination, they demoted me to

the level of a new doctor – fresh out of school. The money was not enough to meet our needs. This was the kind of economic pressure added to the political pressure they applied to someone whom they disliked.

At that time in China, no one could do any work without the permission of the government labor board. All work was assigned and under the control of the government. If you did unassigned work, it was a crime. So Pearl went to the labor board asking for a job as well, because my salary was not enough to keep us alive.

The director investigated her credentials and then said to her, "We need musical specialists, teachers, and other workers in the arts. But you have spent time in prison. Your husband has committed serious political blunders. Also, you resigned from your previous work. If you need work you may choose to stitch leather shoes, become a ditch digger, or do construction work."

My wife asked, "Do you mean that I should give up my training to do something else that I have never known? Is that a right policy?"

He gave her a cynical smile and said, "Political status comes first. We never use anyone with bad political standing even though you have good training. Get out of here! We have work to do."

Our Child – Janet Marie Yeh

In deep distress, Pearl came back and told me the

labor board's harsh words. On the one hand, I consoled her believing that God had allowed us to survive through the valley of the shadow of death and He would provide for us, but on the other hand I was really worried about our future. My wife and I knelt down to pray, clearly knowing that we needed to hold fast to Him and see the deeds of God. Even though people mistreated us, God would take care of us.

A new baby, whom we had asked God to give us, would soon be coming into our home. How could I support all the needs with the small salary that had been allowed me? Was there a future for our baby to grow up under such political domination and economic pressure?

Someone suggested that we have an abortion. But as Christians, how could we agree to do that? Life is from God, and we have no right to destroy it. Furthermore, we wanted to have the baby. My brothers and I were all in early middle life, and there were no children in our whole family.

With tears and some worrying, we asked God to take care of all these concerns. One night I heard a spiritual voice speak to me, clearly and simply. It was the night of September 21, 1972, nearly four months before our child was to be born. The voice said, "Believe and trust." The next morning I told Pearl that God had answered our prayers. "Believe and trust" encouraged us. We lived with that promise until the baby was born.

On January 26, 1973, a new little life came from God and everything went well. God took care of us and my daughter had no special emergencies because she was in good health. My wife was really blessed. There was no fever and no infection so she stayed in the hospital only a few days. We had borrowed money to pay the bill, because Pearl had no health insurance since she had no job. We named the little girl "Believing and trusting." Being so recently frustrated in her own musical career, my wife noticed our little girl's long and strong fingers. She said to me, "Our little girl is blessed by God with a wonderful pair of hands. They will be well-suited for piano playing when she grows up."

As time went by, her skill was evident. We knew again that God keeps His promise to those who believe and trust. Thank God for her wonderful pair of hands. After she arrived in America, she started to serve God through music – performing the piano in over 100 churches all over the United States. Many people have been blessed through her music and we give Him all the glory. His mercy is everlasting and His truth endures to all generations. Glory to His name.

Living Under Suspicion

Because of my political "cap," I was spied on all of the time, even at home. Our neighbor told us that she was given a police device and ordered to record our conversations and to keep track of when we left the house and when we returned. She also reported everyone who came to our home – even our parents and brothers.

In the hospital where I worked, the political leaders never talked to me. They pretended not to see me and turned away their eyes when we faced each other. They looked upon me as a criminal because I had a heavy political "cap." In their estimation, they were as white and pure as snow because they came from the working class.

We knew that two of them, the highest political secretary and his assistant, were living immorally with the young lady doctors and nurses. The assistant was caught one midnight sleeping with a lady doctor in a room of the hospital. When he heard the knocking on the door, he climbed out the window and tried to hide on the roof. When he was caught by the hospital guards who shined their flashlights on him, he only lifted his hands and said, "It is I. I am wrong. Punish me, please."

According to the law of that time, such illicit sexual behavior was simply called, "the problem of life." He was not punished. They said his nature was good because he came from a poor peasant family. His problem was that he had been corrupted by coming in contact with the bourgeois class. After several months, he was transferred to another hospital and was still considered a very good political leader.

Personal morality was not highly valued. Public pronouncements said that stealing, fighting, sexual crimes, drinking, and murder would not break the foundation of the socialistic system. Therefore, such crimes became common all over China. But if anyone spoke out against any government policy, he was punished. He was charged with undermining the foundation of the socialist system.

Lord, How Can I Serve You?

I never voiced my opinions to anyone in the hospital because I knew it was as dangerous as playing with fire. I worked hard everyday, treating my patients.

But sometimes I asked God, "Lord, how can I serve You instead of only helping men? Do these unbelievers realize that I am doing good to them because I love You? Why should I spend my time in secular work, after I have walked through the valley of death for my faith? Shall I give myself to matters that weigh so lightly on Your scales? When shall I be released to share Your messages and to testify to the glory of Your name?"

God taught me patience by reminding me of Paul's counsel to Christian slaves in the Roman Empire. He taught them that limitations of this kind were not life's greatest problems. His counsel was, *"Brethren, let every man, wherein he is called, therein abide with God."* (I Corinthians 7:24) I knew that the Bible taught us a very important truth: *"... whatsoever ye do, do all to the glory of God."* (I Corinthians 10:31) I understood that if I did my daily work for Him, I would be pleasing to Him.

I spent my after work time in research and writing some medical articles, but because of the political discrimination, they were not published. The results of the research were good, but the reports were not used. Some people said, "Doctor, why are you suffering such bad luck? You should ask God to help you, otherwise you cannot keep pace with others. Your schoolmates are much further advanced than you."

It seemed true. And I was hurt when I heard others worrying about my misfortune. But it was not bad luck. I was controlled. My situation was controlled because of my previous political problems. I was deliberately shunned and my work disregarded. I was forbidden many ordinary professional advantages for further learning and development – all because of my arrest and imprisonment.

But as I meditated, an inner voice spoke to me, "When the devil oppresses and makes you unfortunate, it shows that you can be closer to God. Jesus was not successful according to the world's standards. And what apostle was successful, as the world counts success?"

These reflections helped me. I praised God that I was so much better off than when I was in prison. I also told Him that my mind and my will were committed to Him, even if all men were against me.

I had seen enough cruelty, deceit, selfishness, and desire for power and profits that I had no desire for them.

At the same time God showed me how desirable were His love, His righteousness, His gladness, and His peace. I was happy that God gave me insight to choose His way in preference to any other path. He taught me, *"If a man therefore purge himself from these, he shall be a vessel unto honour, sanctified, and meet for the master's use, and prepared unto every good work."* (II Timothy 2:21) I asked God to use me all the rest of my life.

Better Times for China

Mao died September 9, 1976. Four weeks later, on October 7th, the guilty Gang of Four were arrested and put in prison. The dark clouds that covered all of China were beginning to disperse. Life was beginning to return to normal. God was stretching out His righteous hand to correct some of the evils committed by China's leaders. Followers and co-workers of the Gang of Four were being removed from their leading posts. Many of those helpers immediately changed their loyalties and began criticizing their former leaders. These men and women were professional politicians, always grasping for power. They pretended to be civilized and lawful, but their driving ambition was to trample others at will. They still wished to sit in chairs of leadership, even in the name of another kind of politics, if only they could force innocent people to obey them. Such people never change their real minds. We Chinese have a proverb, "It is much easier to move a mountain or a river than to change one's mind."

In October of 1978, the police board was reconsidering my case to see if I had received fair treatment. A leader from my hospital came to the board speaking evil against me. She told the police that I was an unstable man in proletarian politics. Because I had relatives abroad, the hospital did not allow me to do any research work for fear the results of the studies would be stolen. In spite of this testimony, the board agreed that my case had been handled unfairly. When the police board agreed to compensate me for their earlier unfair treatment, this leader immediately changed her position. She came to me and said, "I have gone to the police board many times to urge them to compensate you. You suffered in prison, and after your release from prison you were treated unfairly both financially and mentally."

She then told me that I should be thankful to the Chinese Communist Party and to the Hospital Political Organization. She was clearly suggesting that I should thank her because she had been such a good leader.

On December 18, 1978, I was given full vindication by the police board. I was told by the police, "We have re-examined your whole case and have found no reason to have detained you. There is no evidence to show that you committed serious political blunders. The political leader of your hospital came testifying against you, but her charges are ridiculous. We have decided to give you full clearance. The economy of the whole country has been damaged by the Gang of Four, but we will ask your leader to compensate you with a small sum for the loss of your money and for your lowered salary."

He then handed me the certificate of my vindication.

I thanked God for His mercy. He had given me the promise, "Hold fast of Him and you will see the deeds of God." Now that promise was being fulfilled! I knew that this vindication was in no way from man. God was at work. He had fulfilled the promise that He had given to my wife, *"Thou preparest a table before me in the presence of mine enemies: thou anointest my head with oil; my cup runneth over."* (Psalm 23:5)

The clouds were being blown away and the warm sunshine was coming through. We Chinese Christians were expecting that God's love would shine upon our beautiful land, that Christ's true Church would be established firmly and would grow.

God has kept His word. Even in our land, under very difficult circumstances, Christ has built His church – not of wood and stone, but of faith and sacrifice. There are many good Christians in China. Praise the Lord. Only Jesus knows them all – the living and those who have gone to death for Him.

I remember that years ago in my country, it was

easier to be known as a Christian. But when it costs less, it means less. So, if there is a difference today, if there is some special strength among Chinese Christians, it is because of tribulation. Not tribulation in itself, but because of what God does in the midst of persecution when all you can do is to trust and obey. We know from personal experiences the meaning of Jesus' words, *"Whosoever will come after me, let him deny himself, and take up his cross, and follow me."* (Mark 8:34) We have known something of the Cross. We know some of the pain. We know also that there is no way to follow Him without it. But every cup from above is good – even the bitter. Thank God for the cross and for what He has taught us through it.

11

Led by God

Dr. P.K. Li was my wife's uncle, her godfather, a medical doctor and professor in Shanghai Medical School. He was a devoted Christian. Many hours a day, he would pray to God, until he developed many calluses on his elbows and knees. After he received his doctorate from Cornell University, he came back to China to serve his own country. He was honored and protected by the Chinese government until the Cultural Revolution. He was pulled out of his class and insultingly shoved around by his students. They shouted, "A Western slave and spy from America!" He was also ill-treated by the government and was asked to not teach or see patients, but instead to clean the bathrooms and sweep leaves in streets and pathways.

On his birthday, March 22, 1978, he was fasting and praying about our future. God spoke clearly to him through Isaiah 52:11-12: *"Depart ye, depart ye, go ye out from thence, touch no unclean thing; go ye out of the midst of her; be ye clean, that bear the vessels of the Lord.*

For ye shall not go out with haste, nor go by flight: for the Lord will go before you; and the God of Israel will be your rereward."

Through this scripture, God showed him that He was planning a new life and responsibility for us. Dr. Li suggested that we apply for passports from our country and for visas to the United States. But neither one was easy.

I prayed about the decision, but I was worried because I was responsible for the support of my family. If I applied for the passports, I would have to resign from my job in the hospital first, because the political leaders there would try to hinder my applications. If I resigned and then could not get the passports and visas, what would the future hold for me and for my family? During this period, employment was even more strictly controlled. If one resigned from the government appointed job, it meant that the position would be lost permanently. There would be no chance to follow that profession again. Our life would be even worse.

I dared not take that first step. But Dr. Li encouraged and prodded me with his admonition from the Bible, *"Let not that man expect that he will receive anything from the Lord, being a double-minded man, unstable in all his ways."* (James 1:7-8)

Step of Faith

Finally, believing this to be God's will, I resolutely

Led by God

resigned from my job. But first I asked God to open the way ahead for His glory. My wife and I went to the police board and made application for passports. If we had looked at the surrounding or thought more about our future, we would have worried more than we did. But God taught us another special lesson: When Jesus calls, you "can walk on the water" as Peter did.

Usually, I say about myself: My flesh is as weak as a worm, but when God's power is on me I can stand firmly. Therefore, I wish to expose my weakness to His power and to His favor, in order to receive His power so that I may glorify His name.

At home, I prayed at least five times a day that our passports would be granted. One morning I was praying very earnestly, and the Holy Spirit led me to pray deeper and deeper. Then God told me, "If you put yourself under My omnipotent power, nothing is impossible." I thanked God for His promise and for His almighty power. All that morning I was full of joy and gladness.

But after one month with no progress at all, my old human weakness overcame me and I went out to seek advice from others. I hoped that someone could help me work it out. I thought that I should make some further efforts of my own. I had the time to do it because I was now unemployed. During this time of worry, God showed me a vision one night. In the vision I saw that all of us had received our passports. But even with this assurance, I pushed ahead using my own ways and methods to replace His great power and His deeds. Then a voice from above rebuked and admonished me. "You have tried to rely on man more than on Me."

I understood that this voice was from God, so I knelt down asking for His forgiveness. I regretted that I had been so weak. Fortunately, God corrected my way and His rebuke was strong enough to uphold my weak spirit. He worked it out when I stopped trying to do it in my own way, and rested in faith on His promises. I had no job, no income to support my family. My mother-in-law and my parents were helping us. How long could they support us? My wife also encouraged me not to worry about our future. She reminded me that God had helped me when I was imprisoned. But it was hard. One month had passed, then another and another.

Five months had gone by, when one morning a letter from the police board came in the mail telling us to come for our passports and to bring five yuan each to pay for the balance due to them.

Tremendous! The passports were for my wife, my daughter, my mother-in-law, and me. They had been granted in spite of the past false political files and of a very deep negative attitude in the police board. We were to be allowed to leave. It was a miracle! We praised God for His revealing guidance and thanked Him for His promise: "Hold fast of Him and you will see the deeds of God." I quickly informed my family and they were all happy for us and gave thanks to God.

Visas

Getting the passports was one miracle. But the next necessary step was to secure visas from the American Embassy in Peking. It would require another miracle. Before the visas could be granted, it was necessary to have a sponsorship from someone in the United States.

We had met Dr. Paul Skiles, Dr. Jerald Johnson, and Rev. John Holstead very briefly when they visited China just one month before we got our passports. God had already prepared for us by sending them to China. How miraculous it was! Now we understand why at that time Dr. Skiles' heart was so eager to visit China.

To get the sponsorship from someone in America, we prayed to God for help and direction. Then we wrote letters to our relatives in America as well as to Dr. and Mrs. Paul Skiles. The Skiles quickly completed all required documents and mailed them to us with their kind letter of invitation before we got another sponsorship from our relatives. We thanked God for opening the way before us. We knew clearly that God would do His work for us through our dear brothers and sisters in Him. Then we got permission from a hospital for my advanced study and from a college in Oklahoma for my wife's further training in music.

God's love on earth always needs a human channel – someone who does not just say words, but puts His love into action, even costly action. And they do it joyfully, without limits. Thank God that through the love of Christians, God's messages and our testimonies can be shared with others. Thank God that through the love of His people, He has opened a new life for us.

Before we went to Peking to apply for visas, the weather was very cold. In Peking, it was four degrees below zero, and there was no heat in the trains. Dr. P.K. Li, prayed to God to give him a sign that He would make our journey successful. He prayed for warm weather – that would be the sign. After his prayer, he felt very happy and peaceful in spirit, so he told us to get ready immediately for the trip. Thankfully the weather did become warmer. We stayed in Peking for one week and the weather was pleasant. The sun shone brightly everyday. We had experienced again that *"the effective fervent prayer of a righteous man availeth much."* (James 5:16)

In the waiting room at the American Embassy, we were anxious about getting permission for the whole family. There were three people ahead of us in line, and their requests were for single permission only. Single visas were easier to get because the government's logic was if only one person left China, he/she would be more likely to return and more apt to return quickly, without reservation. They would come back to be with the family members that were left behind. If a whole family goes, there would be no reason for them to return to China. Therefore, to get whole family visas was nearly impossible.

Amazingly, one by one, all three people ahead of us were turned down. I was the fourth in line. At that moment, God impressed my wife to be completely frank and to tell them everything that we wanted. We went in together for the interview and showed the consul all our completed documents. We told him that we were four persons; our family of three and my wife's mother. We wished to visit our relatives and friends in America.

We had been so sure that it would be impossible to get visas for four persons that we had left our daughter and my mother-in-law at home when we came to Peking. We had told our daughter, who was then only seven years old, to kneel every day with her grandmother and pray for us. She was faithful in her prayers for us, but she went further. She had a request of her own. She asked God not to let her daddy and mommy go without her, not to allow us to be separated. And God answered her prayer.

After the consul asked us several questions, we asked him if we could sign the applications for our daughter and for her grandmother even though they were not present. He replied kindly, "Certainly you may sign for them."

Within minutes we had received permission for all four visas. It was God's miraculous power and His gift of love to us. We thanked the consul general and in our hearts we gave praise to God. He told us to return to pick up the visas at four o'clock that afternoon.

As soon as we left the embassy we telegraphed the good news home. But the information got there before our telegram. At 6:30 that morning, a beloved Christian sister had fasted and prayed for our success. As she prayed, God revealed to her that He had answered her prayer and that all four of us would be granted visas and she told our family members. So about eight hours before our telegram arrived, the family had already received the good news.

We returned to the embassy at four o'clock that afternoon, assuming that many persons would be there to pick up visas. But on this day, out of nearly forty applicants, only our family had received visas. As the Chinese officer handed me the visas he said, "The consul general was crazy today. Your family of four persons were the only ones to receive visas. We do not know what he was thinking. We have never before known of visas being issued to an entire family."

Incredible? It seemed so to the clerks, but the impossibilities of man were the possibilities of God. His power overcame all. These miracles have made us understand clearly that: *"Faith, mighty faith, the promise sees. And looks to God alone; Laughs at impossibilities and cries, It shall be done!"*

After we had returned to our relatives' home in Peking, we gave our testimonies to them and together we thanked God for His miracles. Our own words seemed inadequate to express our gratitude to God, so as we knelt down to pray, we sang the words of this psalm set to a Chinese tune. *"Make a joyful noise unto the Lord, all ye lands. Serve the Lord with gladness: come before his presence with singing. Know ye that the Lord he is God: it is he that hath made us, and not we ourselves; we are his people, and the sheep of his pasture. Enter into his gates with thanksgiving, and into his courts with praise: be thankful unto him, and bless his name. For the Lord is good; his mercy is everlasting; and his truth endureth to all generations."* (Psalm 100:1-5)

We also wrote the words of this psalm in a letter that we sent to our family members who had prayed for us. God never denied His promise to us; praise be to His name!

Last Days in China

It was just two days before the Chinese New Year, so we decided to remain in Peking for the holiday with our relatives. It was the first time I had been in Peking. What a wonderful and meaningful New Year it was! Our week in China's capital was a deeply moving experience. It is a large and severe city with many historical remains and famous buildings. The Great Wall attracted and amazed us. China is a beautiful land, but damaged by evil. There are hundreds of millions of beautiful people, all created by God, but many are destroyed in spirit and in body by the devil.

It was with solemn minds and heavy hearts that we prepared to leave our dear land and people. We would be leaving most of our family, together with many relatives and friends. Would we ever return to our dear land and to our people? We prayed that God would someday restore His church in China and that the church would live permanently under His direction. We prayed that God would bless our nation and save our people.

To buy the airline tickets to America was impossible for me. We prayed that God would open the way. It was a painful feeling to ask for help. We borrowed money from our parents, brothers and friends. With this money we bought our tickets to San Francisco, with a stop in Japan – where we planned to visit friends. We were each permitted to take twenty U.S. dollars and twenty-five pounds of luggage for each person. Together for the four of us, we had $100 and 100 pounds of luggage. This was a "mercy" from the government.

My wife and I had a very clear and strong invitation from Dr. and Mrs. Paul Skiles in Kansas City, but it was given before anyone knew there would be four of us. According to our Chinese custom, it would be very impolite to arrive with more guests than the host invited or expected. So these questions came to my mind: Where would we go? Where should we live? Was it possible for me to find a job while I was taking advanced studies in the hospital? I have a wife, a seven year old daughter, and an aged mother-in-law. How could I make a living for them in America?

Question after question crossed my mind, but I

could not answer them. I told Jesus, "You know the whole situation of yesterday, today, and tomorrow. I do not know even the next minute what will happen to us. I know it is not worthwhile to worry about the future, but Lord, please take care of us."

If we had not been trusting God and counting on His mercy, we would not have dared to start the trip. Though we had some close and distant relatives and some friends in America, for the most part we would be strangers in a strange land. Had we worried about the future, we would have been downcast and discouraged. But God had already stretched out His hands to lead us through *"the valley of the shadow of death."* We could trust Him to guide us on our way.

A good Christian sister prayed with us about our future. God revealed His word to her from the Scripture, *"I beseech you therefore, brethren, by the mercies of God, that ye present your bodies a living sacrifice, holy, acceptable unto God, which is your reasonable service. And be not conformed to this world: but be ye transformed by the renewing of your mind, that ye may prove what is that good, and acceptable, and perfect, will of God."* (Romans 12:1-2)

Inspired by the Holy Spirit to comfort us, she said, "Go ahead and fear not. God will take care of all of you." We felt happy because God had given us this assurance. It was a very important lesson for us to know that we should ask earnestly, and then wait for His clear answer before we walked into the unknown.

On March 7, 1980, we were ready for departure. The airplane was waiting to take us overseas. Our family and friends were at the airport. Nearly everyone was silent and serious, but we felt secure in the will of God. We shook hands and hugged each other. There were tears in our eyes as each one sang in his own spirit, "God be with you until we meet again." My mother gave me her precious advice, "My son, step out with faith as did Abraham. God is with you. Don't fear; always pray. God will take care of all of you."

We spent one week in Tokyo, where we were warmly welcomed by some Japanese doctors. They showed us the scenic spots and places of historical interest in Tokyo. We were also asked to visit the Medical Research Center and hospitals. Dr. Kunimasa Kodo took us into his home in Hachioji City, Tokyo. He and I only knew each other through the medical field in China, for we were colleagues. His wife had passed away not too long before and their whole family treated us extremely well. They took us to several of the best restaurants in Japan for dinner. I was told that one day's expense in Tokyo was equal to nine days expense in America.

Although we were politely invited as their important guests, my mind was not at ease while we were with them. I found myself a stranger without a country, without a home, without a job, without land. I had nothing at all. As a feather blowing and floating in the air without knowing where to go or where to live in America: a strange new land.

March 14th, we took a Pam Am plane for America. As we flew across the Pacific, the attendants served dinner. We prayed before we ate, and my daughter was frightened. She nudged her mother and whispered, "Mom, do not forget to pray secretly. Otherwise you will be put in prison again. Remember, you taught me to do this? Why have you forgotten?"

With joy my wife told her, "Now we are free. We can pray publicly because there is no trouble any more. It is a blessing from God. Do not be afraid, my little sweet spirit. Pray wherever and whenever and whatever you wish."

My own heart was filled with praise to God for His faithfulness and His kindness. Psalm 107:13-15 says: "*Then they cried unto the Lord in their trouble, and he saved them out of their distresses. He brought them out of darkness and the shadow of death, and brake their bands in sunder. Oh that men would praise the Lord for his goodness, and for his wonderful works to the children of men!*"

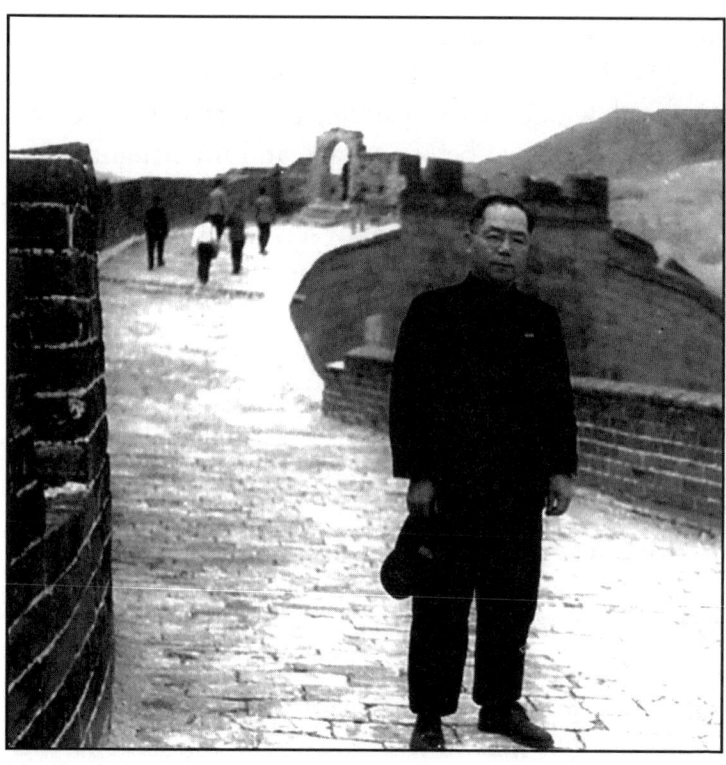

Dr. P.K. Li, my wife's godfather, to whom God spoke through Isaiah 52:11-12, urging us to leave China and to begin a new life in America.

12

America

After a fourteen hour flight, our plane arrived safely at the San Francisco Airport. The beloved Christian brother who had helped my wife during her flight from the authorities was there to meet us. His wife and two small boys came with him. Words could not express our thankfulness that by God's mercy we were meeting each other in America. We decided to stay in their home because we thought they would understand our situation better than relatives and other friends from whom we had been separated for more than thirty years. Eagerly we shared our testimonies of the ways God had led us. They treated us as warmly as though we were brother and sisters.

"What is your next step?" they asked. "Where are you going to live? If you wish to stay with us, for the sake of Jesus, we are willing to let you live and work with us. We will make every effort to help you get your permanent visas."

We asked God to bless this kind Christian family

according to His promise, *"For whosoever shall give you a cup of water to drink in my name, because ye belong to Christ, verily I say unto you, he shall not lose his reward."* (Mark 9:41)

We received a long-distance call from Dr. Paul Skiles and God's plan was made clear again. Dr. and Mrs. Skiles strongly urged us to come to Kansas City and make our home with them. He assured us, "You are all very welcome. Everything has been arranged, so do not hesitate and do not delay."

In our spirits we said, Amen, and decided to go forward. Then more questions came to our minds. Would our American brothers and sisters accept our different customs and culture? Could we adjust? It would be very new and strange for them and us. But we rested in the knowledge that any Christian, anywhere in the world, is God's child. We would be members of the same family in Christ.

Early in the morning of March 19th, our Chinese brother took us to the airport. We hugged each other and said goodbye. Living in America would be a new chapter in our lives.

We arrived at the Kansas City International Airport at 4:30 in the afternoon of March 21, 1980, and were met by Dr. and Mrs. Skiles and some close friends. As we were introduced to each other, Mrs. Skiles gave flowers to my wife and her mother and a small doll to my daughter. How excited we were when Miss Mary Scott said in Chinese, "Welcome friends. How are

America

you?" Then we learned that she had been a missionary to China.

Soon we arrived at the home of Dr. and Mrs. Paul Skiles. Before we entered, Dr. Skiles handed me a house key, on a key ring engraved with the words, "Church of the Nazarene." He said, "This is the key to your new home. It's ours together. Your permanent home where you may live. You are welcome among us. Your coming here is a great blessing."

We thanked God and we thanked them for these kind words. Thus, we began our new life in America – with so many things to learn. Each day, we read the Bible and prayed together. Many Christian brothers and sisters came to greet us warmly and to get acquainted with us.

Freedom to Worship God

March 23, 1980, was an unforgettable Sunday for us who had been lost to public worship for more than twenty years. We went to the Overland Park Church of the Nazarene. Rev. and Mrs. Dennis Johnson welcomed us. As we sat in the sanctuary, my heart was filled with praise, and my eyes were filled with tears. I was seeing the vision fulfilled that God had given to me in the prison hospital. He had shown me that I would worship with yellow and brown-haired Christians. I also remembered that the devil had tried to pull me out of God's love and care. He had told me that I could go abroad and find success in the world if I denied Jesus.

My heart was blessed as I listened to the beautiful choir and the sound of the pipe organ. Pearl whispered to me, "God's promise to me in the vision of a church, just three days after you were released from prison, has been brought to pass. Oh, the music was so beautiful!"

After being starved for public worship for so long, we knew how the Psalmist felt when he sang: "*How amiable are thy tabernacles, O Lord of hosts! My soul longeth, yea, even fainteth for the courts of the Lord: my heart and my flesh crieth out for the living God. For a day in thy courts is better than a thousand. I had rather be a doorkeeper in the house of my God, than to dwell in the tents of wickedness. For the Lord God is a sun and shield: the Lord will give grace and glory: no good thing will he withhold from them that walk uprightly. O Lord of hosts, blessed is the man that trusteth in thee.*" (Psalm 84:1-2, 10-12)

Sharing our Testimonies

Dr. and Mrs. Paul Skiles asked us to stay in Kansas City and seek to be established there instead of going to Oklahoma. We agreed to that. In Dr. Skiles' home, we began to tell how God had helped us while we were in our terrible ordeal. Christian brothers and sisters listened to our testimonies with deep sympathy and tears. God had begun to release His message and the story of His deeds through us. Friends urged us to spend time writing the story to glorify His name.

On Easter, my wife Pearl, my daughter Janet, and I were invited to speak and to perform on the piano at the Mid West Nazarene College Church in Olathe, Kansas. Dr. Rev. Cunningham was in charge. We were told that around 2,000 people would attend to listen to our story and piano solos. My wife was very nervous because she had stopped performing on the piano for more than eighteen years. Her fingers felt stiff and uncooperative, and her mind felt fearful. My daughter Janet, only seven years of age, had never presented herself in front of so many people. I did not know what I should say to such a large audience. My English was not good enough to make people understand everything. Dr. and Mrs. Paul Skiles prayed with us and encouraged us to do our best with the help of God. My wife and daughter started to practice diligently and I also began writing what I should say.

That was the first experience in America. On Easter evening, March 30, 1980, Dr. Paul Skiles and his wife, Maxine, took us down to Olathe. As soon as my wife saw the new building, she shouted with joy saying, "Look, the church building. It is exactly what I saw in my vision almost ten years ago. It is amazing!" We later found out that this building was finished only one year before in 1979, but the church was already shown by God a decade earlier. We fully understand that God controls our future and our destiny. He alone holds tomorrow.

That entire evening service was our program. Dr. Paul Skiles introduced us and the first to perform on the piano was Janet. This was the first time she played publicly and she did a beautiful job. The audience enthusiastically applauded her. Next was my wife. She prayed that God would hold her for His glory after eighteen years of forced silence in music. She performed *Fantasy Impromptu* by Chopin and *Moonlight Sonata* by Beethoven. The audience applauded her with love and support and tears in their eyes. Glory to God for supporting us. My testimony was next and even though my English was not perfect, Christians cried and lifted up the name of the Lord for giving us the power to survive the Cultural Revolution. They recommitted their lives to God.

Another bigger service was scheduled for June, 1980 at the Nazarene Church General Assembly. This time, around 20,000 people attended. We were excited but asked God to help us for His glory. People all over the world came for this service and afterwards, we received letters from Christian brothers and sisters saying that they needed to reevaluate their lives for God. They believed that Christians who lived in the United States were too comfortable and many took God's love for granted and did not do enough work for God's Kingdom. Thank God for His blessings, His love and guidance. He is victorious!

Since then, one by one, invitations from different churches all across the United States flowed into our mailbox. Almost every weekend, the Dr. and Mrs. Skiles, my wife, my daughter, and I began to leave for different cities, towns, and states. I shared my testimony about God's grace, and my wife and daughter performed on the piano. We traveled to thirty-three states, and over one hundred churches, praising God and spreading His Word. God used us to honor His name in America. I have received many letters from those who have heard our story. They testify that through this witness, God is helping them to change their lives and to reevaluate their services for Christ and His church. We thank God for His great plan in which He helped us in our troubles and has worked through us to help others.

We have never stopped sharing our testimonies. Every chance I get and whenever I get an invitation, I travel to that church and share with my brothers and sisters in Christ. As Christians, we have the responsibility to share God's love and Jesus' salvation with believers and unbelievers. We need to win souls and give others the gift that God has given us.

A Little Miracle in America

One night, a patch of hair on the upper left side of my head came out. The Chinese call it, "getting your hair cut by a ghost." We consider it a shame for a man to have a bald spot among these healthy hairs. I prayed to God to give them back. I asked Him with Christ's promise, *"But the very hairs on your head are all numbered."* (Matthew 10:30) I knew that my hairs had been lost and I believed that it was known to God. I believed that He could make them grow again. After several months, the lost hairs came back gradually and completely. I am thankful. Even now, at the age of sixty, I still have all my black hair, without graying. Do you believe that the very hairs of your head are all numbered?

Light for Our Way

The next necessary step for us was to get permission to remain in the United States legally. We did not know how God would open the way for us, and we could be deported if we did not get permission to remain. Also we could not impose on our friends indefinitely. We were thankful to God for His special temporary arrangements and for using us – but we were living a very unusual life. What was the next step?

On May 18, 1980, God revealed a vision to me showing me my future work in America. I saw two church buildings. Around the edges of the roofs were many light bulbs. Suddenly these bulbs lit brightly, but I did not understand what it meant. Then I saw Maxine Skiles standing in front of me. I asked her what it meant. She replied, "It means that you can work now."

Then the vision disappeared, but I was confident

that we were going to be able to stay longer in America. The next morning I told Dr. and Mrs. Skiles about the vision. There were some problems to overcome, but I felt God had answered my prayer. And through this vision, He had shown me that Sister Maxine Skiles had been chosen by Him to help us. We would trust Him for everything.

Nine months later on February 7, 1981, we got permission from the immigration office. Our visas were all changed from visitor classification to Preliminary Work Permission. The vision was fulfilled.

In June of 1980, we had moved to a house that was provided for us for six months by Mr. and Mrs. Roy Davis. They said when they first saw us in the Overland Park Church, God had spoken to them and told them to help us this way. Other Christian friends helped us to move into our new home. They were so helpful and hardworking, and we felt the love of God through these wonderful brothers and sisters in Christ. We did not know how to express our gratitude to them all, but we asked God to reward them for their love and care for us.

In a vision the night of June 10, 1980, God revealed to me that Dr. Paul Skiles was to be a good friend of my spirit. In the vision, he was teaching me to sing a gospel song. The words were, *"Fame and wealth are unreal. Prosperity is vain. We should forsake them all."*

I understood clearly that God was helping me to

learn to take precautions against fame and wealth as I was starting to serve Him in America. At the same time He showed me once again that Dr. Skiles was a good brother and that I could place my full confidence in him when I had any problem.

We are sure that Dr. and Mrs. Skiles were clearly chosen by God to help us, because He gave us two visions concerning them. They love us very much and we love them. We shall esteem their costly love forever. Our circle of new Christian brothers and sisters has grown quickly. We appreciate deeply every good Christian who has shown love toward us.

In America, we have learned many lessons of Christian love. In response we are seeking to learn how to become love channels to those who need Christ's help. May God's love from heaven flow through His children to earth. May His will be done on earth as it is in heaven.

Where God Has Led

I got work as Chinese Ministry Coordinator at the headquarters of the Church of the Nazarene. My wife voluntarily helped me with my Chinese radio broadcasting, as she could speak Mandarin much better and more accurately than I. It was truly a joy to serve God in that way.

But God gave me a vision of three bright lights and told me that He wanted me to serve Him in the field of

Natural Medicine. Back in 1981, not many people knew about Natural Medicine. Whatever the media reported concerning this field, was anything but positive. I was therefore understandably concerned. How could I be a pioneer in this field of medicine? Could I pass the test before the medical board? How would I obtain the finances to open an office? Could I make enough to both support my family and maintain an office? Would people come to me for treatment in a field they were unfamiliar with? Question after question plagued me with uncertainty.

Thank God, He is the Commander and we were His soldiers marching forward to win all kinds of battles. Fortunately we trusted and have devoted our lives to serving Him by helping patients and witnessing God's blessings of creation through His Natural Medicine.

Through the help of Rev. Dr. Don Peterman and Rev. and Mrs. James Shaw, I made a trip to San Francisco to take my Natural Medicine test. I was one among forty who passed, out of the 500 applicants. Three month later I received a license from the California Medical Board of Assurance. Because I had a California license, I obtained permission from the Kansas Medical Board to practice in that state along with Dr. Sharp. It was there that we established the first Yeh Center of Natural Medicine, Inc. Truly God's calling was right and perfectly timed. Many patients, unable to find help from the conventional medical field, were greatly helped by Natural Medicine.

Rev. Dr. Don Peterman called me from Upland, California from time to time asking that we move there. Feeling that this was a call from God, we decided in 1982 to go. There we set up our second corporation, Yeh Center of Natural Medicine, Inc. and then our third corporation, Natural Medicine International, Inc. for treatments and products. Since my wife received her Ph.D. in Chinese Natural Medicine in 1984, we have been working together at our center in Upland. But in cooperation with my associates, we still maintain our Kansas office for the patients in the Mid-West.

God is love, because He knows clearly that people need a real medicine from His creation. He has put us here to help a great many patients suffering from years and years of treatments and medicines that are the products of man's wisdom, rather than God's. Natural Medicine is truly the classical medicine for it has its origins in the Bible.

Having now established ourselves in Upland, our daughter Janet, who was then twelve years old complained of loneliness at not having either a brother or sister as her classmates had. Since I was already nearly fifty and my wife in her early forties, we prayed seriously concerning this matter. Our prayers were answered in that God gave us twin daughters, Beth and Becky on May 1, 1986. We considered this no small miracle. It was truly a double blessing.

Our oldest daughter, Janet, studied molecular

biology and graduated from the University of California in San Diego in 1995. She then went on to study Natural Medicine and passed her license test in 1997. She now works with us and is studying for her Ph.D. in Nutritional Science.

Janet's fiancé, Kevin Huang, is another blessing God has brought to our family. He is the general manager of New Life International, a division of Natural Medicine International, Inc. He is a law student and when he has completed these studies will go into Natural Medicine.

In America, from the first day of our arrival until today, we have seen a lot of its greatest parts and also the darkest parts. We thank God for His bountiful blessings upon this beautiful country, but a lot of people take it for granted. They don't give thanks and glory to God. Instead they have turned away from His ways to walk in sinful paths. We must pray for them and for this country which has been so good to us.

Dr. Paul and Maxine Skiles, our friends and sponsors, on the occasion of our becoming American citizens in August of 1989.

My oldest daughter, Janet, in 1987 blessing audiences by her artistry as a concert pianist.

13

Growing Through Suffering

There are many kinds of suffering, but every pain can be profitable to those who believe in Christ.

Some Christians suffer as a result of former sins. Although this is suffering of low value, God wants to ease the pain and make it profitable to us. We may recall how much greater our sorrow would have been if we had not found Christ when we did. Thus, even this suffering can be a part of God's discipline that He uses to help us share His holiness.

Some will not leave their evil ways until sin brings such suffering that they realize their error. Thus they are moved to forsake their sinful ways. God uses His rod to discipline men and to turn them into His ways of righteousness. If we meet this kind of trouble, let us not be stubborn or stiff-necked. Let us examine ourselves under His light and humbly confess our sins. *"If we confess our sins, he is faithful and just to forgive us our sins, and to cleanse us from all unrighteousness."* (I John 1:9)

Sometimes suffering comes so that God can purify and strengthen us before He uses us. Before Joseph became the ruler of Egypt, he suffered bitterly. It is always difficult to understand this kind of suffering at the time that it occurs. We cannot foresee the future and thus cannot know what God is getting us ready to do for Him. We are inclined to sigh because of our misfortunes. But we can be sure of this: if God allows trouble to come, He plans for us to be victorious in the struggle. He gives us His promise: *"But the God of all grace, who hath called us unto his eternal glory by Christ Jesus, after that ye have suffered a while, make you perfect, stablish, strengthen, settle you."* (I Peter 5:10)

At times suffering comes to us as a means of testing. Sometimes God tests us to know whether He can trust us to be faithful to Him under greater stresses than we have thus far known. Many people today, like the 5,000 who were fed by Jesus, follow Him for His loaves and fish. They follow Him for His earthly blessings and for His help with their earthly needs. God is concerned about these needs. But in our discipleship Jesus wants to lead us beyond material blessings. Until we get beyond living for the things of this world, we are not yet true disciples of Christ. Our goal as Christians is to know Christ in His fullness, to follow Him, to think His thoughts, to do His work, to suffer – if needed, and to see His work accomplished. Can we say with Paul, *"Yea doubtless, and I count all things but loss for the excellency of the knowledge of Christ Jesus my Lord...*

That I may know him, and the power of his resurrection, and the fellowship of his sufferings, being made conformable unto his death." (Philippians 3:8.10) Only when we are thus ready to suffer with Him can Christ say to us as He said to Peter, *"... upon this rock I will build my church; and the gates of hell shall not prevail against it."* (Matthew 16:18)

I will be frank and tell you that I did not always know Jesus as well as now. Suffering has opened my spiritual eyes and sharpened my spiritual ears to understand Him more clearly. That new understanding is a blessed experience. To confirm it and enlarge it, I often repeat the prayer of Psalm 139:23-24: *"Search me, O God, and know my heart; try me, and know my thoughts; and see if there be any wicked way in me, and lead me in the way everlasting."*

In the past, China had many Christians in name but not so many in fact. When suffering came and there were no material benefits from the church, many turned quickly to worldly power. The number of church members dropped. But by suffering, the real Chinese church has been purified. It now stands firmly on the Rock, Jesus Christ. The church has been established more firmly than ever before because of her suffering. There are many faithful and respected Chinese Christians. We appreciate and love them all. Trials could not destroy the church because there was an inner strength from God to support and to uphold every faithful Christian.

If you are a Christian, but you still are not quite sure that you can stand firmly upon the Rock, would you ask Jesus to show you the way? If you feel that you could not remain true through suffering, would you ask God to draw you closer to Him? If the trial is too heavy to bear, God is merciful and He will open a way for us to go. He will not lead us into trials that are outside of His plans and that cannot add to our strength. After the trial has gone, our spiritual life will be stronger. We shall find ourselves willing to cast aside some things that we once thought we could not give up. We shall be so purified that our communion with God is closer than ever before.

Therefore, let us be at ease when we are suffering. Let us believe and trust Christ fully. If we do not lose our faith, we shall not lose our strength. This faith is the difference between believers and unbelievers. We believers have strength in our spirit, therefore, we have peace. God promises us, *"... as thy days, so shall thy strength be."* (Deuteronomy 33:25)

Suffering Persecution

Persecution for the sake of righteousness seems uncommon in Christian lands today. However, across the centuries many have suffered for doing good. They have been persecuted for protecting the innocent and resented for challenging injustice. Jeremiah called the Jews to repent for disobeying the commands of God.

But his king not only refused to obey, he arrested Jeremiah and put him in prison. John the Baptist reproved Herod for the sin of marrying his brother's wife. For this, John was put in prison and then beheaded.

These men of God suffered for the sake of righteousness. They were persecuted because they spoke out against wrong. They did not fear the authority of evil rulers, and they would rather support the truth than protect their own lives. But the prophets knew their job. God had set them to be guardians of righteousness. Others might keep silence but they could not. Jesus praised these faithful prophets and supported their action when He said, *"Blessed are they which are persecuted for righteousness' sake, for theirs is the kingdom of heaven."* (Matthew 5:10)

Persecution for the work of Christ and in the name of our Lord is the most valuable form of suffering. Every Christian should have some share in these experiences. If our Christian faith does not bring us into conflict with evil or worldliness, perhaps our lifestyle is not enough like that of Jesus. He tells us that at the end of the world, *"Then shall they deliver you up to be afflicted, and shall kill you: and ye shall be hated of all nations for my name's sake."* (Matthew 24:9) There are Christians in many lands today who know that not all such persecution lies in the future. We are not to seek for suffering, but we are expected to be aggressively Christian – and we are not to shun suffering, when following Christ brings us into conflict with a world that opposes Him.

There is a gladness in our spirits when we suffer for the name of Jesus. Such joy comes in no other way. God may console us when we suffer from other causes, but only he who suffers for Christ finds both consolation and happiness. Peter could testify, *"If ye be reproached for the name of Christ, happy are ye; for the spirit of glory and of God resteth upon you..."* (I Peter 4:14) Jesus says, *"Blessed are ye, when men shall revile you, and persecute you, and shall say all manner of evil against you falsely, for my sake. Rejoice, and be exceeding glad: for great is your reward in heaven: for so persecuted they the prophets which were before you."* (Matthew 5:11-12)

Finding Peace by Living in Christ

Renouncing self in the face of trouble and drawing back into Christ brings His peace. The real reason that we suffer when we are in trouble is that we still have desires and love for ourselves. Those who die with Jesus may have trouble but they have no pain. Pain is from inside, but trouble is from outside. Too often we try to get rid of trouble by changing the environment. But in doing this, we only replace our present pain with another one. Trouble can be released sometimes by human efforts, but pain of the heart is cured only by God. In every time of trouble Christ promises, *"These things I have spoken unto you, that in me ye might have peace. In the world ye shall have tribulation: but be of good cheer; I have overcome the world."* (John 16:33)

Many Christians have not let their faith really transform their lives. They have accepted Jesus as Savior but have not made Him Lord and Senior Partner. They may read the Bible and pray, and they may even go to church. But if you live close to them, you find that their lives have not been changed. They are not yet living *in* Jesus.

Before we find this closer fellowship with God, we are self centered. Even our Christian life revolves around ourselves. We believe in Jesus because we wish to gain eternal life. We study or work hard because we want a comfortable life. Sometimes we pray very earnestly because we hope to get what we need for ourselves. In making our decisions and solving our problems, we rely on ourselves. We seldom ask God what is His will for us. We have come to know Christ, but we are not yet living *in* Him.

In this relationship to Christ, we are subject to failure and sin. Because we do not rely on His guidance we sometimes do wrong without knowing it. Because we do not rely on God's power we sometimes know what is wrong but we are not able to overcome it.

How can one be a Christian for many years and his life still not be basically changed? The answer is that we need to go deeper with Christ. It is good to begin the Christian life, but it is bad to stop short of full commitment to God and to fail to live in full fellowship with Him.

How do we move ahead from knowing Christ as Savior to the deeper level of making Him Lord of our lives? The change occurs most often when we hear Bible teaching on entire sanctification. Having heard that message, we respond to Jesus' command to tarry until our lives are filled with His Holy Spirit. If we have not heard this Bible teaching, God can lead us into this deeper Christian life as we respond to His voice. That is how God led me into this life-changing experience.

One day we find ourselves in a situation where we know that we must have more help from Jesus than we have ever had before. We cannot follow His way in our own strength. In this hour, we earnestly ask for His deliverance.

At that time God opens our inner eyes, and His light comes into our hearts in a new way. We can now understand Him more clearly, and we rely more fully on His power. Our spiritual eyes are opened and we know clearly the way He wants us to go. We are amazed at how little we saw and how dark it was before our inner eyes were opened. We repent and ask God for forgiveness for our weakness and failure. We confess our need for a closer walk with Him. We ask Him to show us what He wants us to do. If we are fully open to His will, He shows us our need and He fills us with His Holy Spirit.

This deeper encounter with God is followed by real

life changes. Our thinking, our speaking, and our doing will be quite different from what they were before. We understand more fully that there is no grace or blessing or deliverance or hope without Jesus. Living in Him, we find His peace, His happiness, His fellowship, and His guidance. It may seem something of a mystery until we experience it, but it is real. Of his own experience Paul writes, *"I am crucified with Christ: nevertheless I live; yet not I, but Christ liveth in me: and the life which I now live in the flesh I live by the faith of the Son of God, who loved me, and gave himself for me."* (Galatians 2:20)

Living *in* Christ means listening to what God says and obeying what He asks. I thank God that He led me personally into this experience. If we had not found this deeper life with Him, we would not be alive today.

Praying in the Spirit

Sometimes I am asked, "How can we get the words directly from God? How does God reveal His will through visions?"

First, I wish to say that this form of revelation is a gift from God and He gives His gifts to different persons in different forms. He may also reveal His will, to us in different ways.

However, we know that God is a revealing God. He wants to have fellowship with us and to make His will known to us. He has revealed himself in many ways.

Before we had a written Bible, God said, *"If there be a prophet among you, I the Lord will make myself known unto him in a vision, and will speak unto him in a dream. My servant Moses is not so, who is faithful in all mine house. With him will I speak mouth to mouth, even apparently, and not in dark speeches; and the similitude of the Lord shall he behold: wherefore then were ye not afraid to speak against my servant Moses?"* (Numbers 12:6-8)

But in our day we have the Scriptures and the teachings of Jesus. Even so, the Bible usually gives us only general or universal guidelines. Only God himself can show us His special will for our individual lives. For this purpose, He sent His Holy Spirit into the world, and He sends Him into our lives. Jesus promised, *"Howbeit when he, the Spirit of truth, is come, he will guide you into all truth..."* (John 16:13) He wants us to know. He invites us to ask. He assures us that His Holy Spirit will lead us.

It is not ours to dictate how God's Spirit shall reveal His will to us. It is ours to ask for His guidance. It is His sovereign decision to choose how He brings certainty to our spirits. You may receive your guidance in ways different from mine.

But there are conditions that we must all meet if we are to receive God's gift of guidance. If we wish to pray in the Spirit, we must live in the Spirit. We must be sure that our spirits have been cleansed by His blood. Jesus promised His followers, *"If ye abide in me, and my words abide in you, ye shall ask what ye will, and it shall be done unto you."* (John 15:7) It is a staggering promise, and we do not know all that it means, but of this we are sure: if we are to receive guidance from Him, we must abide in Him.

The second step is to pray in the Spirit. God is a Spirit; we communicate with Him spirit to Spirit. My personal experiences of praying in the spirit have made me very happy and peaceful. God was so near and so real to me that I was not willing to stop praying.

I have learned that it takes time to come to God in spirit. It is impossible to experience Him in this way by praying only a few minutes. If God is to communicate profoundly with us, we must spend much time in His presence. We Christians are servants of God. We need to pray for God's work, for other Christians, for lost souls, for our country, and for the whole world. All need our love and support through prayer.

Why do I emphasize spending much time in prayer? Because I have learned that we cannot overcome our enemies except by keeping close to Jesus, our Lord. If we are not close to Him, we are in danger every hour. The Bible exhorts us, *"But ye, beloved, building up yourselves on your most holy faith, praying in the Holy Ghost, keep yourselves in the love of God..."* (Jude 20-21)

The Worth of His Word

God tells us, *"Blessed is he that readeth, and they that*

hear the words of this prophecy, and keep those things which are written therein: for the time is at hand." (Revelation 1:3) I testify that this verse has been true in our lives. As we have learned His will from the Bible and have followed His guidance, we have been released.

His Word is sweet! Before I was put in prison I read the Bible every day as a part of my schedule. Sometimes I read it carefully but sometimes I read it hurriedly. I did not realize how fortunate I was to have God's Word until we lost the Bible. In China at that time, it was illegal to read a Bible or to sing a hymn. There came to us the feeling of hunger and thirst for His Word, such a feeling I had never known before. We had come upon the day of which the prophet wrote: *"Behold, the days come, saith the Lord God, that I will send a famine in the land, not a famine of bread, nor a thirst for water, but of hearing the words of the Lord."* (Amos 8:11) I regretted that I had not memorized many more verses and chapters. I recalled from memory as much of God's Word as I possibly could. But it was never enough. I loved the Word that I had because it was so sweet, but I had lost God's Book.

I knew a Christian who traded his watch for a New Testament. In that farming area a watch cost a year's salary. At the same exchange rate a small New Testament would cost $10,000 in U.S. dollars. Chinese Christians value the Bible. We have experienced the bitterness of losing God's Word, so we have known the sweetness of recovering the Bible.

I have never heard of a person crying tears of joy when he recovered a lost book, but I have seen such an outpouring of emotion from a strong man when he got a Bible – even a small one – after he had been deprived of God's Word for more than ten years.

His Word gives courage! When everything is peaceful, we are usually not so aware of our need of help from God. But we turn to Him in the time of wind and storm. Therefore God does not allow His children to live always in a pleasant environment. It is better to find God in a storm than to lose Him on a sunny day. In my trouble, I began to know God's voice and to understand the importance of obeying His Word. If I had not heard His voice, I could not have tolerated my suffering in jail. That Word became my life and my strength. No other voice in the world could have saved me at that time.

His Word is powerful! God's Word can support and console a broken heart. Without the help of God's words of guidance, I would have gone out of my mind in the jail. Without the help of God's Word, my wife and I would not be alive today.

Without the help of God's revelation to His Chinese children, all the lights in China would have gone out during the darkest and hardest times there. Without His help, the Chinese church would not have survived. But thanks to our God, because of His powerful Word, His church in China is growing and prospering. Because He is with His church, and because His church has His word, *"...the gates of hell shall not prevail against it."* (Matthew 16:18)

His Word is faithful! Jesus is the same yesterday, today, and forever. So is His word. He never breaks a promise, and He never loses His power. By His Word the heavens and the earth were created; everything in them is under His control. At the end of the world even the heavens and the earth will pass away, but not one dot or one dash of His Word will be changed. His Word is faithful and will remain so forever. His truth endures to all generations because He cannot deny Himself.

If you have met with some things that you do not understand, believe and trust Him. Do not worry or be doubtful because He will not fail you. This is my testimony.

14

The Battle with the Devil in America

I know that the battle with the devil is not limited to the kind of trials that we went through in China. I have known some Christians who stood firmly in hard times but they went down in easier days.

The church in Symrna (Revelation 2:8-11) suffered fiery tribulation. It was a violent form of Satan's attack, and they stood firmly against it. But the church of Laodicea (Revelation 3:14-22) failed because they had it too easy and the people were too self-satisfied. Laodicea was the only one of the seven churches that received no commendation from Christ.

The church at ease is in great danger because the world easily comes into such a church. The children of God then follow the trends of the world, the church compromises, and the people almost unconsciously become like the world.

1) The battle against money and being a "workaholic." Many people in capitalist countries work hard for money, which has no value to God. To work hard for God is good, but if we work all day long and decrease our devotion hours, this is not right. We must find a balance between devotion, work, education, rest, and sleep. Too often we become Martha – working all day long, when all God wants from us is to listen, obey, and learn from Him. Just like Mary, we must sit at Jesus' feet and hear His Word. *"Martha, Martha, thou art careful and troubled about many things: but one thing is needful: and Mary hath chosen that good part, which shall not be taken away from her."* (Luke 10:41-42)

2) The battle against ease. A Chinese proverb points out, "One can often survive through hardships, but never survive ease." Many times, I have noticed many Christians that are caught up in entertainment, resorts, restaurants, shopping, theaters, games, plays, movies, tapes, and adult temptations. Because everything is so easy to obtain, many brothers and sisters get caught up in the world and secular activities. It clearly states in the Bible that even though Christians are in the world, we are not to become a part of the world because our eternal home is with God in heaven.

3) The battle against laziness. God wants us to have a balance in life – devotion, work, education, rest, and sleep. Because jobs are so easy to get and quit, welfare so easy to get on and off, many become lazy and don't do their fair share in society. Some people live off of the system. This is not right. In the book of Genesis, when man sinned, God clearly said that only through hard labor, can one eat and survive. As Christians, we must maximize our God given abilities and utilize our capabilities.

4) *The battle against sinful sex.* Sinful sex is legal in the United States and many children and teenagers grow up thinking that to sleep with multiple partners is a part of life. Sex education is taught to children at a very young age – giving the false propaganda that sex is permissible as long as it is "safe sex." Fornication and adultery are sins and are wrong according to God's laws. Marriage is a gift from God and each of us who are married is blessed with a special partner for life. We must be loyal, faithful, committed, and loving toward our spouse.

5) *The battle against the multitude.* As Christians, we cannot travel the way of the multitude. Peer pressure to do drugs, smoke, drink, party and have casual sex is so strong. It is hard for young people to not follow their friends and therefore they choose incorrectly. They need God's help. Parents, begin early to discipline your children down the right path. They will encounter enormous peer pressure as they grow up, and the only way for them to remain morally strong is to have a strong spiritual foundation. The allure of the world is strong and the path to destruction is wide, and those who find it are many. But on the way to heaven, the path is narrow, and those who find it are few.

The devil has many faces, but he has only one purpose. Whether by the violence of persecution or by the seduction of an easy life, Satan proposes to draw us away from God.

6. *The battle against the individual.* The horrible age of the individual is coming, if it is not here already. People are so independent, so self-centered, and so isolated. There is very little heartfelt love, a lack of caring, no warmth, no deep friendships and a lack of genuine worship of God. The apostle Paul described it best when writing to Timothy: *"This know also, that in the last days perilous times shall come. For men shall be lovers of their own selves, covetous, boasters, proud, blasphemers, disobedient to parents, unthankful, unholy, Without natural affections, trucebreakers, false accusers, incontinent, fierce, despisers of those that are good, Traitors, heady, highminded, lovers of pleasures more than lovers of God; Having a form of godliness, but denying the power thereof: from such turn away."* (II Timothy 3:1-5) *"But evil men and seducers shall wax worse and worse, deceiving and being deceived."* (II Timothy 3:13)

7. *The battle for our children.* Satan is the destroyer and he seeks to destroy no one more than our young people. He has an arsenal of various means that he uses such as abortion, illicit sex, drugs, rebellion, suicide, gangs and the list goes on. We must remember what Paul told us: *"Be sober, be vigilant; because your adversary the devil, as a roaring lion, walketh about, seeking whom he may devour: Whom resist stedfast in the faith, knowing that the same afflictions are accomplished in your brethren that are in the world."* (I Peter 5:8-9)

On this earth, the devil presents himself as a roaring lion before all Christians, young and old. This means he wants to overcome you, to tear you to pieces and then eat you spiritually, mentally and physically. To overcome him we must, *"Submit yourselves therefore to God. Resist the devil, and he will flee from you."* (James 4:7) In order to have the devil flee from us, we must resist him, but in order to do that, we must be submitted to God. And we will only be submitted to God when we are truly a born again child of God.

Ask yourself, "Am I born again?" Jesus tells us in His Word: *"Verily, verily, I say unto thee, Except a man be born again, he cannot see the kingdom of God."* (John 3:3) At some point in time, you must confess your sins before Jesus Christ, acknowledging that you are a sinner, incapable of earning your way to heaven, asking for His forgiveness and cleansing, trusting in His finished work on the cross as your only way of salvation and accepting Him as your Lord and Savior. *"... now is the accepted time; behold, now is the day of salvation."* (II Corinthians 6:2) Instantly, you will clearly know you are not the same as before. You are changed. You will receive a new life, and the Holy Spirit will come and take up His abode within you, to be your Comforter and Guide, and help you overcome the attacks of Satan. *"Therefore if any man be in Christ, he is a new creature: old things are passed away; behold, all things are become new."* (II Corinthians 5:17) *"What? know ye not that your body is the temple of the Holy Ghost which is in you, which ye have of God, and ye are not your own? For ye are bought with a price: therefore glorify God in your body, and in your spirit, which are God's."* (I Corinthians 6:19-20)

Some may argue that they have been born into Christian families, they go to church every Lord's Day, they've been educated in a Christian school, they believe in Jesus and read their Bible everyday. This is very good, but this is not being born again. To be born again is a sovereign work of the Holy Spirit, Who regenerates our spirit by imputing to us the righteousness of God in Christ Jesus, thus enabling us to live a holy life here on this earth and to be able to go to heaven hereafter. There is no other way. We cannot earn our way to heaven by our good deeds outweighing our bad deeds, so to speak. It is Christ's way which leads to eternal life or our way which leads to eternal death. *"… choose you this day whom ye will serve;… but as for me and my house, we will serve the Lord."* (Joshua 24:15)

15

Faith and Final Words

As Christians, we must go forth and spread the Good News unto all the nations, educating them about the Kingdom of Heaven. We need to teach unbelievers how to find forgiveness for sins, eternal salvation and sanctification. We must live according to what we preach, because our actions can either win others to Christ or lose them. We must educate them about faith because by faith, we can gain access to Jesus Christ. God gives Christians this promise, as stated by Paul in Romans 5:2. But what is faith and is only having faith enough for a non-Christian to be saved?

Faith is a word with many meanings. It can mean faithfulness, *"Who then is a faithful and wise servant, whom his lord hath made ruler over his household, to give them meat in due season? Blessed is that servant, whom his lord when he cometh shall find so doing. Verily I say unto you, That he shall make him ruler over all his goods."* (Matthew 24:45-47)

Faith can mean absolute trust, as demonstrated by

the Roman centurion who came to Jesus asking for healing of his servant and Our Lord said of him, *"... I say unto you, I have not found so great faith, no, not in Israel."* (Luke 7:9)

It can mean confident hope, *"Now faith is the substance of things hoped for, the evidence of things not seen."* (Hebrews 11:1)

As James points out, it can even mean a barren belief that does not result in good deeds, *"What doth it profit, my brethren, though a man say he hath faith, and have not works?... But wilt thou know, O vain man, that faith without works is dead?"* (James 2:14, 20) Our faith must express itself in helping others.

In Romans, Paul talks about faith, but we must be very careful to understand faith as Paul uses the word. Faith is not something we can or must do in order to earn salvation. If that were true, then faith would be just one more deed, and Paul clearly states that human deeds can never save us, *"Knowing that a man is not justified by the works of the law, but by the faith of Jesus Christ, even we have believed in Jesus Christ, that we might be justified by the faith of Christ, and not by the works of the law: for by the works of the law shall no flesh be justified."* (Galatians 2:16)

Even in the Old Testament times, grace, not deeds, was the basis for salvation. As Hebrews 10:4 points out, *"For it is not possible that the blood of bulls and of goats should take away sins."*

Instead, faith is the gift God gives us because He is

saving us, *"For by grace are ye saved through faith; and that not of yourselves; it is the gift of God."* (Ephesians 2:8) It is God's grace and not our faith that saves us.

By His mercy, He gives us faith when we receive His salvation. Through the faith He gives us, He carries us from death into life, *"Verily, verily, I say unto you, He that heareth my word, and believeth on him that sent me, hath everlasting life, and shall not come into condemnation; but is passed from death unto life."* (John 5:24)

We need to have faith, but it is important to know exactly what it is. It is God's gift to us when we repent of sins, turn from our wicked ways, and follow Him with our complete heart, soul, mind, and body. When we put His will and His way above our own, and find true eternal salvation, He awards us with faith so that we may have a one-on-one relationship with Jesus Christ. Then, God will help us to become more like Christ, *"… that ye may be perfect and entire, wanting nothing."* (James 1:4) This is the Good News that we need to share with others. We must accept His gracious gift, and allow Him to plant the seed of faith within us.

Final Words

I trust that our lessons of blood and tears have been a help to you but I ask you to forget the persons in the book; look only upon the One who led us through the *"valley of the shadow of death."* Ask Him to lead you also just where He wants you to go. Ask Him to reveal Himself to you – to reveal His reality, His goodness, and His purpose for your life.

A Chinese sister said, "Naturally, no ones wishes to be imprisoned, but if that were necessary to enjoy Christ's sweetness and His presence, I would be willing to remain in jail." Chinese Christians are still fighting strongly against the devil in their spiritual war. They need the support of your prayers and your remembrance. Please pray for them, and ask God to give them strength to overcome the evil one.

Christians in our age at the end of the world should prepare for darkness. There will be many tribulations and destructive heresies. Let us watch and pray, asking God to help us. Let us trust and obey His Word. Let us love each other fervently from the heart. Let us gird our minds for action, keep sober in spirit, and place our hope completely on the grace to be brought to us at the revelation of Jesus Christ. Let us sacrifice ourselves for Him. Jesus tells us, *"Verily, verily, I say unto you, Except a corn of wheat fall into the ground and die, it abideth alone: but if it die, it bringeth forth much fruit."* (John 12:24)

Recently I have been taught by His voice to my spirit, "Before you are taken up into glory, you must keep on going the way of the cross, as Jesus did when He was on earth."

I believe that He is coming again very soon. I ask you to be challenged by His Word, *"I beseech you therefore, brethren, by the mercies of God, that ye present your bodies a living sacrifice, holy acceptable unto God, which is your reasonable service."* (Romans 12:1)

The following words of Scripture have often supported me. From my own experiences, I bear glad witness that they are true. I testify to the power of these sweet Words, which were the only things that I could survive on in my darkest hours. They were my strength and my shield.

"This is a faithful saying, and worthy of all acceptation, that Christ Jesus came into the world to save sinners; of whom I am chief." (I Timothy 1:15)

"If we believe not, yet he abideth faithful: he cannot deny himself." (II Timothy 2:13)

"This know also, that in the last days perilous times shall come. For men shall be lovers of their own selves, covetous, boasters, proud, blasphemers, disobedient to parents, unthankful, unholy, Without natural affection, trucebreakers, false accusers, incontinent, fierce, despisers of those that are good, Traitors, heady, highminded, lovers of pleasures more that lovers of God; Having a form of godliness, but denying the power thereof: from such turn away." (II Timothy 3:1-5) I have seen much of this, and I know its danger.

"But call to remembrance the former days, in which, after ye were illuminated, ye endured a great fight of afflictions; Partly, whilst ye were made a gazingstock both by reproaches and afflictions; and partly, whilst ye became companions of them that were so used. For ye had

compassion of me in my bonds, and took joyfully the spoiling of your goods, knowing in yourselves that ye have in heaven a better and an enduring substance. Cast not away therefore your confidence, which hath great recompence of reward. For ye have need of patience, that after ye have done the will of God, ye might receive the promise. For yet a little while, and he that shall come will come, and will not tarry. Now the just shall live by faith: but if any man draw back, my soul shall have no pleasure in him." (Hebrews 10:32-38)

"But without faith, it is impossible to please him; for he that cometh to God must believe that he is, and that he is a rewarder of them that diligently seek him." (Hebrews 11:6)

"… In the world ye shall have tribulation: but be of good cheer; I have overcome the world." (John 16:33) God has proven this to me.

"And they overcame him by the blood of the Lamb, and by the word of their testimony; and they loved not their lives unto the death." (Revelation 12:11) He has done this for us.

Dear Reader, *"Wherefore seeing we also are compassed about with so great a cloud of witnesses, let us lay aside every weight, and the sin which doth so easily beset us, and let us run with patience the race that is set before us, Looking unto Jesus the author and finisher of our faith; who for the joy that was set before him endured the cross, despising the shame, and is set down at the right hand of the throne of God."* (Hebrews 12:1-2)

"Worthy is the Lamb that was slain to receive power, and riches, and wisdom, and strength, and honour, and glory, and blessing." (Revelation 5:12)

"Great and marvellous are they works, Lord God Almighty; just and true are thy ways, thou King of saints. Who shall not fear thee, O Lord, and glorify thy name? for thou only art holy: for all nations shall come and worship before thee; for thy judgments are made manifest." (Revelations 15:3-4)

"When you pass through the waters, I will be with you; and through the rivers, they will not overflow you. When you walk through the fire, you will not be scorched, nor will the flame burn you. For I am the Lord your God, the Holy One of Israel, your Savior." (Isaiah 43:2-3) To these blessed truths we say Amen and Amen.

Our Commitment

O Lord, we will follow You anywhere that You lead us. You are our Master.

"Who shall separate us from the love of Christ? shall tribulation, or distress, or persecution, or famine, or nakedness, or peril, or sword? Nay, in all these things we are more than conquerors through him that loved us." (Romans 8:35, 37)

OUR HEART'S DESIRE

I'd rather have Jesus than silver or gold;
I'd rather be His than have riches untold;
I'd rather have Jesus than houses or lands.
I'd rather be led by His nail-pierced hand.

I'd rather have Jesus than men's applause;
I'd rather be faithful to His dear cause;
I'd rather have Jesus than worldwide fame.
I'd rather be true to His holy Name.

He's fairer than lilies of rarest bloom;
He's sweeter than honey from out of the comb;
He's all that my hungering spirit needs.
I'd rather have Jesus and let Him lead.

Than to be the King of a vast domain
Or be held in sin's dread sway.
I'd rather have Jesus than anything
This world affords today.

Rhea F. Miller

Faith and Final Words

My parents came to America in September of 1988. Both died within a few months after being here, my mother in August of 1989 and my father in May of 1990. My brother John, a cardiologist on the East coast, is seated next to my father.

My blessed family: Kevin Huang, Janet's fiancé, my wife's mother, our twins, Becky and Beth, Pearl, myself and Janet.

Pearl and I relaxing in our patio at home.

Yeh Center of Natural Medicine, Inc.; 195 N. Second Avenue; Upland, California 91786.   (909) 946-6444 1-800-998-8919